Buying a Business

Also in Right Way

The Right Way to Start Your Own Business
Book-Keeping The Right Way
Reading Between the Lines of Company Reports
The Right Way to Write Reports
The Astute Private Investor

Buying a Business

What you must know

by

David Stokes

RIGHT WAY
plus

Typeset in 10pt Legacy Serif Book by Letterpart Ltd., Reigate, Surrey.

Printed and bound in Great Britain by Mackays of Chatham.

The *Right Way Plus* series is published by Elliot Right Way Books, Brighton Road, Lower Kingswood, Tadworth, Surrey, KT20 6TD, U.K. For information about our company and the other books we publish, visit our website at www.right-way.co.uk

Dedication

This book is dedicated to my lovely wife Suzanne who has been so loving and supportive over more than 37 years of very happy marriage.

Acknowledgements

It is impossible to write a work of this nature without help and assistance from many friends and associates.

I would like to thank in particular:

John Anderson for the original inspiration.

My wife Suzanne for putting up with my many hours glued to the keyboard, and the all too frequent exclamations of frustration. She also undertook to proof-read the text, mainly to check that it made sense, but also along the way to correct all my lapses in grammar and spelling.

John Anderson, John McGarry (business transfer agents), Ann Hall, Geoff Hall (financial advisor) and Peter Rose (banker) for giving me the benefit of their many years of experience in their respective fields by making invaluable comments and suggestions concerning the technical and practical content of the text.

And Lucy and Chica for frequently delaying walkies!!

David Stokes

Contents

About the Author

David Stokes was born in England in 1944. Apart from four years in Singapore, he has worked in the UK all his working life.

Initially, David worked in banking, holding a number of management positions in domestic and international banks. Much of his time was spent assisting new business projects to get off the ground.

In 1988 he left the City to work for himself. Together with his wife, David has run a number of small businesses in the past fifteen years, including one in retail, a care home and a computing services operation helping small businesses. He has also assisted a number of others to establish their own businesses, including franchises in three business sectors.

This is David's first book, but it has been a project that has been in his mind for a number of years. David has felt for a long time that there is a need for a basic, but comprehensive, guide for first-time buyers of businesses. Now he has finally been able to find the time to bring this project to fruition.

Introduction

Over the course of my business life I have come across countless people with aspirations to run their own businesses, but without the confidence to take the plunge. It has always seemed to me that there is a crying need for an easy-to-read, step-by-step guide on how to go about deciding whether to look for a business opportunity and, if so, how to proceed.

When I began my career in the 1960s the commonly held belief was that large employers with their structured career paths represented the most secure employment. When I went for my first interview at Barclays Bank in Luton I was told that, provided I kept my fingers out of the till, I would be offered a job for life. No personnel officer could legitimately make such a promise today. The fact is that many talented people, who thought they had a secure job, find themselves redundant in the prime of life through no fault of their own. Perks such as the company pension scheme and car are no longer worth what they once were.

It is arguable, therefore, that running your own business can be the more secure option. After all, small businesses have always been the backbone of the British economy and remain so today. When you are your own boss your destiny is much more in your own hands, and you will fully benefit from the fruits of your labours.

However, buying a business, particularly for the first time, is not something that should be undertaken lightly. Careful thought and planning is needed. I have therefore written this book to assist anyone thinking about buying or starting a business. I have tried to make it as comprehensible as possible, not too detailed but containing most of the key issues that a first-time buyer should consider. The subject matter has, I hope, been organised in a logical order, taking the reader through the decision-making process in the natural sequence that issues will arise.

It has to be said that it is not right for everyone to run a business, and in the first chapter we explore some of the considerations to be taken into account when deciding whether it will suit you. A few people will feel after reading the first chapter that it doesn't and will decide that there is no point in reading on. However, most aspects of running any business are mainly a matter of common sense, and a logical approach to acquiring the business in the first place will eliminate most of the worry.

Professional advice is available for all the key areas of the business – legal, accounting, banking, insurance, etc. Most of these professionals offer their advisory services to assist in the identification, set-up and purchase of your new business. However, whilst I do not rule out seeking such advice at the early stages, I am adamant about one piece of advice that I will give. DO NOT RELY ENTIRELY ON PROFESSIONALS IN REACHING THE DECISION TO BUY OR ESTABLISH A BUSINESS. Remember, hardly any of these professionals have any experience in running a business other than their own practice. Seek guidance by all means, but thoroughly investigate and analyse the opportunities for yourself. Hopefully, by the time you have read this book you will have all the basic knowledge you need to do that with confidence.

Note: To avoid continual use of phrases such as 'he or she' and 'his or her' throughout the book, I simply use the terms 'he' and 'his' to refer to both men and women.

Chapter 1:

Should You Be Buying a Business?

As stated in the Introduction, most business management is a question of exercising good common sense. If you have taken the trouble to obtain this book, then you clearly already have the interest, maybe a keen interest, to own and manage your own business, and presumably you would regard yourself as possessing the necessary common sense. These two attributes are the first and foremost prerequisites to success.

The rewards from successfully running your own business, generally speaking, are far greater than you will enjoy as an employee. I suppose that the fact that you are your own boss, and all the profits are yours, would be the most quoted reasons for wanting a business.

However, the rewards can be much more than just that. I have found from my own experience that there are immense satisfactions apart from the financial rewards. It is very pleasing to see a business grow and develop under your control. My wife and I have always run businesses together, and our first business acquisition after I left the City was a rather rundown care home with thirteen residents (down from nineteen) and a rapidly dilapidating building. We implemented a planning permission that was already in place, and as a result the whole building was refurbished and enlarged. The home became fully up-to-date in terms of facilities and the capacity increased to twenty-six. We sold the business in 1990, some four years later, and I admit we made a worthwhile capital gain, as well as enjoying a good income in the meantime. However, we look back with much pleasure at the achievement of the refurbishment (which was not easy to organise around a business looking after thirteen frail elderly people) and the many good relationships we developed with the staff, residents and

11

families. The improvements we made to that business gave us a great sense of achievement and satisfaction, to a degree that neither I nor my wife had ever experienced in employment.

I am not suggesting that all businesses are like our care home, but with the exception of businesses that are mail-, Internet- or telephone-based, most involve human relationships of one type or another. As the boss, you will on occasions get the flack, but generally you tend to be much closer to the customers than you will have been as an employee, and treated on a more respected basis by people from all walks of life.

So, yes, running your own business can be very rewarding, but what attributes must you have to be successful as a business owner?

Willingness to work hard

Many people say, 'Work smart not hard.' We have all heard of people who have found 'nice little earners' which bring in the money for little effort. Most multi-level marketing schemes are sold to you on the basis that once your down-line network is established, the commission will simply accrue without any effort on your part. Have you ever met any successful multi-marketing people who do not work hard? There are plenty of people who have developed their business to a point where they can take long holidays and work whatever hours they wish, but they have always had to work hard over a considerable period of time to get the business to that point.

The simple fact is: ninety-nine people out of a hundred who run their own business work hard and always will.

Ability to take pressure

As the boss, the buck always stops with you, and whatever problems arise will ultimately need to be solved by you.

Capability to be decisive

All decisions will need to be taken by you and, if your business is to be successful, you cannot be one of life's procrastinators. If you do not stock the new line being offered by the sales representative, it will be offered to your competitors, so you must be able to take a quick and decisive view on whether or not it is a winner.

Have a flexible attitude

The world is constantly changing. The business that is locked in the past will die. You must go with the flow to succeed. I remember going to a bank cocktail party where the new Business Banking Centre was being opened by the owner of a large and successful department store in the town. In his speech he proudly joked how he had declined to accept debit cards, which at the time were the latest payment system just introduced by the banks. He obviously didn't see the need to suffer the bank charges involved, when he knew his customers would buy from him anyway.

What do you bet you could pay by debit card there now!

Be willing to learn

There are several aspects to this. Most people coming out of an employed position, to run their own business for the first time, will have skills in certain areas, but running a small business entails dealing with every aspect of the business. Even if you have staff or contractors to do various tasks, these people quickly recognise a boss who is completely ignorant of the issue at hand and often take advantage.

Every type of business has basic elements that you must get right if the business is to do well. It could be location or maybe stock control. Possibly it is efficient factory layout or reliable delivery systems. Unless you have recently worked in the type of business you are buying, you will need quickly to identify and understand these key issues.

As stated already, you need to be flexible towards change, and obviously this can involve learning new skills.

Ability to deal with people

This attribute is as important as any.

When you work in a large organisation you often tend to deal mostly with people at a fairly similar level and in similar fields to yourself. When you run your own small business, you will have to deal with a variety of people at a variety of levels.

The successful businessperson is able to motivate people, whatever their relationship to the business, whether it be:

- Senior employee.
- Junior employee.
- Important owner/employee of a client.
- Lesser employee of a client.
- Bank manager, tax or VAT inspector.
- Sales rep.

If it is, say, a convenience store you are buying, then all your customers, being local, may well be of a generally similar background and as such you may feel that handling people is not a major concern. Nevertheless, you will still need to be able to communicate with them in a way that makes them feel valued.

If you have the type of business where you need to make sales calls, then you must have the communication skills necessary to present yourself to potential buyers in a way that gives them confidence, both in yourself, as well as your business, to provide the standard of service they require. Do not underestimate this. People buy people first. If you need help to hone your communication skills, then get it.

Equally important is the ability to motivate staff. If they like you and respect you, they will want to pull for you, and you will find that this will make all the difference when you are in a tight corner, or trying to impress a new client to win a first big order.

Franchises

A franchise is where you pay a fee to an established company for an exclusive territory, training, ongoing management backup and support to trade as part of a proven business.

For those dubious about buying a business of their own for the first time, a franchise can be the ideal answer. You are given training in all aspects of the business, help is always available whenever needed from a head office, and you are part of an established and proven operation. As such, you are in business working for yourself, but not by yourself, and success is assured provided you work to the system and put in the effort.

Well, that is the theory, and it can be correct. A franchise can be the ideal solution for people who are unsure that they have the knowledge to jump straight into business on their own. However, like all things in life, some are better than others, and Chapter 3, Looking at Franchises, deals specifically with assessing franchise opportunities.

Business Link

At various points throughout this book there are references to facilities and resources of information available at your local *Business Link*. There is a network of *Business Link* offices around the country which provide invaluable services to existing local businesses and to people thinking of going into business. At this point you should be aware of what this organisation is about and what it can do for you.

Business Link is part of the Department of Trade and Industry. Wherever you live, you will find one fairly near to you, and they run a very good website (see Appendix 4) at which you can view and download many of their publications.

In addition to producing a wide range of publications on just about every aspect of running a business, they also have a library of business books and run seminars, training and special events, and can also effect introductions to useful contacts in most business fields. You can subscribe to their newsletters on whatever subjects are of interest to you, such as IT, Marketing, Health and Safety, Employment, Import/Export and so on. Many local banks, accountants, solicitors and other professionals work closely with *Business Link* so you can gain access to whatever help you may need.

Whilst the offices are usually rather large and imposing, there is no need to feel intimidated. They are there to help the novice as much as the experienced businessperson, and accordingly you will always find them very friendly and helpful.

Once you are in business they are able to offer a lot of advice, and will send out a business consultant to spend some time with you to identify the strengths and weaknesses of your business and where you could benefit from expert help. The initial consultation is always free and they will often then approve a budget for a certain amount of further free help. Once your free time is used up you will have to pay for additional assistance, but the cost is well documented in advance. In many cases the free advice is enough to get you on the right path.

Business Link is a tremendous resource for any budding businessperson and you cannot contact them too soon.

Self-assessment questionnaire

In Appendix 1 you will find a self-assessment questionnaire. It is strongly recommended that you take a few minutes to run through the questions and answer them honestly. As you will see, it is not about aiming for a pass mark. Rather, it is intended to provoke an in-depth self-analysis to clarify in your mind what your strengths and weaknesses are in respect of many of the key aspects of running a small business. Some people will conclude that running a business is not for them. They, at least, will have reached a sensible conclusion at the right time to enable them to go forward in another direction. For most people, however, it will encourage them to go ahead with acquiring a business, but will highlight any areas where they need to consider strengthening their skills.

Chapter 2:

What Type of Business Should You Buy?

This is almost one of those 'How long is a piece of string?' questions. It is, however, something that should be given a lot of thought.

No two people will have exactly the same skills, aims, ambitions or financial resources, so it is impossible to provide a single solution for everyone. However, this chapter presents the key issues that need to be thought about, and will assist you in thinking it through in depth before embarking on your search for the right opportunity.

What are your skills?

All of us have skills in one area or another, and obviously your particular skills need to be taken into account when deciding on a business to buy. At the most simplistic, if you have worked in a certain type of business for someone else, say a hairdresser's or confectioner's for example, you probably have most of the skills needed to run a similar business yourself. If, on the other hand, you have worked in a job that has not provided you with particular skills relevant to running a small business, you will need to consider businesses that do not require skills only acquired after years of training. Consider what skills you would have the capability and aptitude to acquire quickly.

What skills and aptitudes are required?

Some businesses require only generalised skills, and others more specialised ones. It is impossible to give a comprehensive list, but here are some examples to illustrate the point.

Running a small sandwich bar or 'greasy spoon' is very much like running an overgrown family kitchen. That's not to say that it is easy, but learning to scale-up what you already do at home would be relatively straightforward. On the other hand, running an *à la carte* restaurant is a totally different ball game. If you have been a chef, then fine. However, if you will have to rely on employing a chef, then you are taking a huge risk. What happens if the chef leaves overnight without warning? It would take years, if ever, for you to be able to step in and take over the kitchen at short notice.

Running a small convenience store is generally straightforward, but like the *à la carte* restaurant, you could not consider buying a specialist butcher's shop unless you are trained.

Slightly less obvious is accounting requirements. A retail business, where the customer pays at the point of sale, is fairly easy to run with a simple cash book. However, if you are running a business-to-business trade, where your customers expect trade credit, then you are going to need to run ledgers with your customers' accounts, send out statements and follow up by phone, letter and in person to chase late payment.

If it is the type of business where it is necessary to submit detailed quotations, is your English good, your maths OK and are your fingers quick on the keyboard?

In summary, when you consider types of businesses, think about how you will need to be spending your day, and whether you can manage or learn all the tasks you will have to undertake. Possibly your partner will be able to cover your weak areas.

What are the physical demands?

One factor which is easily overlooked is the physical demands that many businesses place on their owners/operators. If you have been working in an office, sitting at a desk all your working life, when you run a shop standing on your feet all day you may find that you have terrible back pains.

Do not under-estimate this. Your immediate reaction to the previous statement may be, 'Well, I will have a chair at the till like they do in Tesco's.' But the problem is that in Tesco's, if the cashiers need a leaky carton of milk to be changed, or more change in the till to finish with the current customer, they ring a bell and someone else appears and deals with it. In the average shop it does not work that way and you will have to lock the till and rush off and back again yourself!

In the pub, when you had planned that your husband would be responsible for changing the beer barrels, if a regular is waiting for a bitter and hubby is at the bank, you are going to have to do it yourself.

All retail and restaurant/café type businesses, as well as many others, involve a considerable amount of physical work. Man or woman, you need to consider whether you are ready for this and whether you are going to be able to cope with the physical demands that may be involved over a sustained period.

How much risk is involved?

All businesses involve a certain degree of risk, and this is discussed in more depth in the next chapter. However, some businesses are more inherently risky than others. You need to decide:

- What risks can you handle, given your aptitudes and skills?
- How much risk are you willing to take?

For the purposes of this discussion, risks can be broadly categorised as external risks and internal risks.

External risks

External risks refer to risks external to the business itself. These risks are largely outside your control once you have bought the business, and can include all or some of the following:

LOCATION

Some businesses are very sensitive to location (hotels or general retail, for example). You can obviously check what you think of the location before you buy, but there can always be environmental changes after you have bought the business that you could not have anticipated, and which fundamentally affect the business. Your hotel, which was nicely situated on a busy road, is now in a back street due to the new bypass. The handy public car park next to your convenience store has been sold to Tesco's. It could be even simpler – the council decides to put double yellow lines in front of your parade of shops.

Technology

Changes and enhancements to existing technology could affect your business. Many small garages are unable to service some of the latest cars which have sophisticated computer and electronic systems.

New gizmos may appear and reduce the demand for your services. Digital cameras are increasingly reducing the demand for photograph development and printing, for example.

Competition

Apart from the increasing trend towards out-of-town major outlets, maybe someone will just decide to open up in competition just down the road.

Fashion

Some things just simply fade.

Customer loyalty

Sometimes customer loyalty is lost when a business changes hands. See the paragraphs on Consultancies at the end of this chapter.

Internal risks

Internal risks are essentially within your control, provided you have the aptitude and attention to detail to exercise it. Such risks could include:

Stock

Do you have the intuition to stock the right items, the hot sellers, or might you end up with shelves of unwanted items?

Debtors

If you are selling to other businesses on credit, will they all pay you? Can you chase and control the slow payers?

FINANCIAL CONTROL

Sometimes staff can think up the most ingenious ways of slipping cash out of the till or stock into their handbags.

You need to consider which are the risks involved in the type of business you are considering, and which of these risks, given your circumstances, you are prepared to take.

Remember – if you are to be a businessperson you have to be prepared to take some risk. Why not? It could be that you are actually taking more risk by being an employee. Hundreds of people are losing jobs through no fault of their own every day of the week!

How much will the business cost?

Chapter 4, How Much Should You Spend on a Business?, deals with the issues of how to assess your financial circumstances to determine the sort of level of investment that is wise for you.

However, this chapter would not be complete without mentioning that the general cost of businesses in any sector must have a bearing on whether it is a business sector you should look at. To take the extreme, if you have a maximum of £10,000 in ready funds to invest, it is hardly worth looking at nursing homes or hotels, for example. On the other hand, a leasehold flower shop may be a realistic possibility.

Trade publications

Most businesses have trade publications. Find out which are the best ones for the types of businesses you are thinking about buying. Read a few issues. They are generally a good source of information, not only for commentary on the major concerns currently affecting that business sector, but will also contain advertisements for specialists in stocktaking, financing and so on.

Talk to business owners

It is a good idea to talk to business owners in the sectors you are targeting for their thoughts. Do not be shy about this; most business people are only too happy to talk about their business to prospective owners, as long as you make it clear that you are not about to open up nearby and put them out of business, of course! However, most business transfer agents (agents who act for owners wishing to sell their business, see page 42), accountants, bank managers or solicitors can give you contacts if you prefer.

Having read this chapter, sit down and consider all the issues. This should give you the ideas and questions to put to them, and, as the conversation develops, the least you will gain will be confirmation that your expectations are correct. But, more likely, you will learn a lot of new aspects to running that type of business that you would have never thought about on your own.

Ask them what key factors there are to making the business successful or not. All businesses, without exception, have a few key factors that you have to get right for the business to do well. For example, some of the key factors in the success of Pizza Hut are:

- Consistent product quality and price.
- Speed of service.
- Easy parking.
- Clean environment.

This sounds obvious, but a considerable degree of skill goes into ensuring that your pizza and chips are exactly the same whichever restaurant you go to. However, it is the knowledge that you can be assured of this that encourages you to go to Pizza Hut time and again, so it is vital for them to get this right.

Other examples are:

- Pubs: Keeping the beer in good condition;
                            Keeping sticky fingers out of the till.
- Convenience stores: Keeping the food fresh and
                            presentation good.
- Flower shops: Avoiding undue wastage.

The key factors in your particular business could concern presentation to the public or more internal factors, like financial control or avoiding undue stock losses, for example. By speaking with existing owners you should gain a good feel for what these critical factors are, and be able to assess whether you have the ability or willingness to make sure that you get them right.

Consultancies

Businesses such as insurance brokers, advertising agencies, graphic designers, IT consultants and the like are often built up through personal relationships that go back over a long time. The same applies to hairdressers. As such there is often a real risk that once the current business owner leaves, a significant number of clients will decide it might be a good time to look around at alternatives.

In many such businesses there is a similar risk in relation to key employees. Instances where employees leave, either to start on their own or to join a competitor, and take clients with them, are commonplace. Practices such as graphic designers or advertising agencies, for example, where the employee works very closely with the clients and has an in-depth knowledge of their likes and dislikes, are particularly vulnerable in this respect. Often if you lose the employee you lose the client, even if the employee doesn't take the client with him, because it was solely for the skill or imagination of that employee that the client used this firm.

If you are thinking of buying a business of this nature, you will need to consider these risks very carefully and, if necessary, consider ways in which you can reduce them. You may need to contract the vendor to stay on in an advisory capacity for a period after take-over, and/or incentivise key employees. You could also consider negotiating to defer part of the purchase price, making it only payable if sales meet projected targets over, say, the first two years after takeover.

It is never possible to eliminate the risks entirely and for that reason these types of business rarely sell for high prices unless they are large practices where the risks are widely spread over a large client base and workforce.

Unless you are experienced, you should obtain specialist advice about valuing such businesses and negotiating contractual terms. The relevant professional institute should be able to offer help in this respect.

Chapter 3:

Looking at Franchises

Buying a franchise can be the right initial business for people who have never run their own business before, but like all business purchases it must be approached with caution and a lot of careful thought.

This chapter will give you a good overview of how to approach choosing a franchise. However, before committing to buy a particular franchise you are strongly recommended to contact The British Franchise Association (BFA) or visit their website (see Appendix 4), which contains a lot of very useful information and advice as well as recommended reading matter. You should also seek advice from a solicitor or other professional advisor, preferably one affiliated to the BFA.

It is possible to buy a brand-new franchise from the franchisor, or to buy an established one from an existing franchisee who has decided to sell. This chapter begins by assuming you are setting up a brand-new franchise outlet, and concludes by dealing with buying an established franchise business. Even if you are looking at buying an established franchise business, you should read the entire chapter.

Let's deal with the theory first, and then tackle how to check out an individual franchise opportunity to see how good it is in reality.

What is a franchise?

A franchise is a licence offered by an existing well-established business (the 'franchisor') to others (the 'franchisees') to operate a similar business using the franchisor's fully developed business model, often trading under its brand-name in a defined exclusive territory. In return, the franchisee agrees to operate the business systems imposed by the franchisor and pays an initial fee. Thereafter the franchisee pays commission to the franchisor, usually calculated as a percentage of sales. Many well-known names offer franchises including McDonald's, Benetton, Prontaprint, Body Shop and others.

What are the advantages of buying a franchise?

As a franchisee you are operating under the wing of the franchisor and will usually benefit from:

- Using a fully proven business model.
- Trading as a well-known brand.
- National advertising arranged by the franchisor.
- Comprehensive training.
- Help with initial set-up.
- Ongoing help and support.

Who is suitable to be a franchisee?

Franchisors target people who have a desire to work for themselves but, possibly never having done so before, would feel more comfortable to have a guiding spirit watching over them to reduce the risks.

All the issues discussed in Chapter 1 apply equally to franchises. Although the franchisor is there to train you, provide all the systems, and give you ongoing support, it is down to you whether or not you are successful.

Like all other business ventures, success in a franchise will require a businesslike approach, hard work and commitment. If you are in doubt as to whether you have these qualities, don't go for a franchise just because you think the franchisor can solve all the problems. He can't and he won't.

The other factor to consider with a franchise is this. The success of the franchisor and all the franchisees as a group depends on everyone following the system and maintaining the standards. Therefore, if you become a franchisee you will have to accept that the way you work, what you sell and how you charge will be dictated by the franchisor, with very little discretion for you to make variations. This is totally understandable. Every franchisee would lose out if each McDonald's or Body Shop you went into was different. Indeed, the most successful franchises are the ones where the franchisor maintains the closest control. After all, their success depends on the customers always knowing exactly what to expect, whichever outlet they happen to visit. However, for the very entrepreneurial franchisee it can become very frustrating not to be able to make changes or diversify without permission, and to be bombarded with directives from head office, so you must be sure that you can work under these conditions before you buy.

What types of businesses are franchised?

The best way to find out if there is a franchise that is potentially suitable for you is to get one of the franchise magazines. There is a wide range of franchises available including:

Professional services

Expenses analysis for businesses (analysing gas, electricity, telephone, etc., for potential savings).
Dating agencies.
Employment agencies.
Travel agencies.
Business transfer agencies.

Delivery services

Parcels, pet foods.

Retail

Shops.
Supplying shops with greetings cards, batteries, children's rides, slot machines.

Cleaning

Domestic cleaning services, contract cleaning.

Repairs

Windscreens, car body paint chips.

What does a franchise cost?

There is an initial franchise fee, followed by a commission usually calculated as a percentage of sales.

Franchise fee

The amount of the initial franchise fee can be as low as a few hundred pounds or as high as hundreds of thousands of pounds, depending on the type of franchise.

The amount will depend on how well established the franchisor is and what you are getting. If you are joining a group like Body Shop, for example, they will be identifying premises, negotiating leases, fitting out, stocking up, as well as training you to run the operation. The fee is therefore going to be tens of thousands of pounds. A franchise for providing domestic cleaning services, on the other hand, will involve little capital expenditure and therefore should be a lot cheaper at a few thousand pounds.

Ongoing charges

Franchisors normally charge for their ongoing support by way of taking a commission on sales. The percentage will vary from case to case.

The franchisor will often also levy a charge for out-of-pocket expenses such as advertising.

Items such as stationery and uniforms will also have to be paid for, where applicable, usually with a mark-up for the franchisor.

What are the disadvantages of a franchise?

You probably decided on a franchise to overcome lack of knowledge or confidence in the early days. The main disadvantages are in the longer term:

- As time passes, franchisees become fully acquainted with the business and begin to feel that they do not need the franchisor. The ongoing commissions and levies become irksome.
- The lack of flexibility.
- The feeling of being like an employee rather than an owner.

- If you want to sell the business, there is usually a fee to be paid to the franchisor, who also has to approve your purchaser.

How to assess a franchise

Buying a franchise is like buying any business: you must do your homework. Franchises are not always what they seem.

All franchisors begin by sending you an information pack. This pack should set out all the major features of the franchise, and should be carefully read before any meeting is arranged. The key issues you are looking at are:

- How much does it cost?
- What do you get by way of training, equipment, supplies, customers, etc., for this fee?
- What is the ongoing support – advertising, marketing, accounting, product, helpline, etc.?
- What are the income projections?

The information pack should include general information about the franchisor, including a general history and how long it has been in business, as well as the number of franchisees currently in the network. It should also include details of its accountants, solicitors and bankers.

There should also be a detailed description about how the franchisees work on a day-to-day basis, which will give you an idea as to whether you will enjoy it.

The only way to assess whether a franchise is value for money is to check it against the other franchises in the same business. It will also be a question of whether you feel the financial rewards adequately reflect the effort and money invested.

If you like the idea and feel it is worth taking further, then you will need to arrange a meeting to begin the process of checking it all out.

Checking it out

The information pack will probably look very impressive. Nevertheless, however good it may look **take nothing at face value**. As has already been stated at the beginning of this chapter, let's look at the theory first and then see how to investigate how good an individual franchise opportunity is in reality. The principles in franchising are fine for those people they suit, but beware. Quite frankly, whilst there are many good ones, a lot of franchises are a waste of money.

These are some of the steps you should take before you commit to proceed:

Speak to The British Franchise Association

There is no law that says a franchisor must belong to any organisation, but most of the leading franchisors are affiliated to this one. The organisation has no real statutory teeth to control franchisors, and is in no way an ombudsman for franchisees, but it has established codes of conduct for its members to follow and, as stated at the beginning of this chapter, is a must to contact before any commitment is made.

Talk to the competition

Even if you have decided that one company looks much better than the others, it is worthwhile having at least a phone call, if not a meeting, with a couple of others before the meeting with the favourite. Ask them why their opportunity is better than the one you like. You can then tackle your first choice about the issues they bring up to see if they can satisfy you. If not, perhaps you haven't selected the right one!

Check the income projections in detail

Even if you have never looked at business projections before don't be afraid to look into the figures. Preparing business projections is largely down to common sense. Go through the income and expense lines, one by one, to understand what assumptions they have used in arriving at the figures, and consider whether they sound reasonable to you. Obviously every business will be different, but let's take an example to demonstrate in general how to approach the assessment of the projections. The example is not based on any detailed knowledge of the business in question, but is intended simply to demonstrate the approach.

Let's take the assumed sales of a small takeaway pizza business. The franchisor's projections show sales building up to

£21,000 per week. Is this figure reasonable?

Well, let's consider the average sale price of a takeaway pizza: £7 seems about right. That means that to achieve weekly sales of £21,000 we will need to sell 3,000 pizzas. If the business is open Monday to Saturday for 10 hours per day (say 2 hours at lunch time and from 5 pm to 1 am in the evenings), then there will be 60 trading hours per week. This means that the projections assume, on average, 50 pizzas are sold per hour, which in turn means many more at peak times. Does this seem realistic? We would have to consider the location and size of the premises but it would not be anywhere near realistic in a small pizza takeaway. It is doubtful that the ovens would have the capacity even if there were the demand. If the projections had assumed 10 per hour in the quieter times and 40 at the peak hours, we might feel more assured of their achievability.

A similar common-sense approach would need to be taken in reviewing the expenses. If wages are shown as £200 per week that would represent 40 hours of hired help at £5 per hour or 20 hours at £10 per hour. Thinking about the amount of help needed, and the going rate for the job, it should be a simple matter to decide if the projection is realistic.

Look through each line of the income and expenses taking a similar approach.

At the meeting with the franchisor, ask him to go through with you in detail how the income projections are calculated, in particular in any areas where you are not clear.

Ask how many franchisees have achieved these projections, and more importantly how many haven't.

Ask about the existing network of franchisees

How many franchisees are there? How many have joined each year to date and how many have left? Why do they leave? What is the range of incomes achieved? How many successful resales of franchises have there been?

Ask about the training

How long is the training course? What is the curriculum? Who gives the training? Is there any hands-on training as well as in the classroom? Is there a follow-up with you afterwards? Ask for a quick sight of the detailed operating manuals. Do they look comprehensive enough?

Ask to speak to existing franchisees

The franchisor should be happy to give you the contact details for, say, three existing franchisees. You should call them to ask whether they are happy with the franchisor, the support they get, and how their income has matched up to expectations. If you are allowed to choose which franchisees to call so much the better, although most franchisors will want to ask their franchisees first, before giving their names out, and this is fair enough. However, if you suspect that you are being given the names of the pet franchisees, you will need to be wary.

Check the franchise magazines

The franchise magazines run interesting articles from time to time and you may find some useful information, especially if you can check back numbers. However, do not expect to find too many negative articles on particular companies – the publishers make their money from the advertising revenues from the franchisors.

Speak to your bank

All major banks have franchise departments, and will have details on file of most franchises. You can usually speak with them direct. However, banks never like to say much in case they are sued, and the franchise department will often be very guarded about what it says. Nevertheless, your local small business manager will be able to speak to the franchise department and should be able to give you an idea as to whether they would lend money for the purchase of that franchise. You could ask him to take a bank reference for you. It won't say much, and a positive one won't necessarily mean much. However, a negative one would definitely tell you to steer clear.

Check at Companies House

If the franchisor is not a household name, you can check it out at Companies House. See Appendix 4 for details of their website.

Free of charge you can do a search on the company name or number (by law these must appear on the official notepaper of the business), and this will show the date the company was formed, and whether the accounts and annual return are up-to-date. For a small fee, you can download the latest annual accounts. This will provide a check on how well established they are, and how financially sound.

Choose a good solicitor

Most franchisors will not vary their standard franchise agreement. This is quite reasonable given that they cannot have different franchisees on different terms. However, you should have a specialist solicitor check out the agreement you are being asked to sign, so that he can at least explain it to you so you know exactly what you are letting yourself in for. If the agreement is unreasonable, he will advise you.

Franchises are a specialised area, and you should find a solicitor with appropriate expertise, preferably one affiliated to the BFA. If your usual solicitor cannot recommend one, they do advertise in the franchise magazines and are listed on the BFA website.

Buying an established franchise business

When you buy an established franchise business you will need to follow all the steps described in the following chapters for assessing how much you can afford to spend, assessing the business and calculating what you think the business is worth. However, because it is a franchise there are extra factors to consider:

Check out how well the franchise works

You will need to carry out all the steps covered earlier for checking out the franchisor and how well the franchise works.

You should be given profit & loss account figures for a number of years (at least two preferably) which, if reliable, will show you how profitable the business has been. Hopefully a large part of the risk has been taken away by the fact that the business has been established and proved to have made money. However, you will still need to satisfy yourself that the franchisor/franchisee relationships are good, and the support provided adequate, because you are new to the business and will need support at least as much as the vendor did when he started. You will need more support in a way, because the business is already up and running, so there is no gentle early build-up. You will be expected to go on the training course, and will need that to be good, just as much as the vendor did.

The vendor is not going to tell you he is selling because he is fed up with the franchisor, or with working hours twice as long as he had been told, so you need to speak with other franchisees in just the same way as you would if you were starting a new franchise outlet.

Check the value

When you buy a new franchise from the franchisor, the fee is fixed and you take it or leave it. However, when you buy an established business the vendor will expect an enhanced price based on the proven profitability of the business and the goodwill created thereby. Obviously there will be scope for negotiation, and you will need to satisfy yourself that you are paying a fair price. To do this, you will need to value it in accordance with the techniques covered in Chapter 6, How to Assess What a Business is Worth.

The difference compared to a non-franchise business is the fees payable to the franchisor. The franchisor will expect to approve you as the new owner, and will normally charge some or all of the following fees:

- An administration fee for checking you out.
- A training fee for your training course.
- A legal fee for entering into a new franchise agreement with you.

In my view these fees, with the possible exception of the legal fee, should be paid by the vendor, or deducted from the agreed sale price.

Negotiating the deal

In addition to signing the franchise agreement with the franchisor, there will be a sale/purchase agreement with the vendor. You may wish to negotiate additional support from the vendor, and other terms. Please read Chapter 8, Negotiating the Deal, for further details.

Appoint a good solicitor

As stated already, you should use a specialised solicitor, preferably affiliated to the BFA. Please also read Chapter 12, Arranging Contracts, for further information.

Chapter 4:

How Much Should You Spend on a Business?

The aim in this chapter is to give you some basic thoughts to enable you to decide how much you should be prepared to invest in a business.

There are two aspects that need to be covered:

- Deciding how much it is right in your circumstances to consider investing.
- Assessing how much of your own money will be needed to ensure your business venture is well funded.

In order to give yourself the best chance of success, it is clearly vital to ensure that you are on a sound financial footing from day one.

There is nothing difficult about working out a sound structure for your finances – it is all down to common sense and, as long as you give this subject the time and thought it deserves, you should have no difficulty in avoiding arguably one of the biggest causes of business troubles: inadequate or inappropriate finance.

In business, as at home, there is nothing worse than forever struggling to make ends meet. You do not want to find yourself held back at critical times by lack of adequate funds. By ensuring that you are well funded, you can avoid the sort of situation where, for example, you know that more business is there for the taking, but you can't afford the extra stock; or where stock has to be run down because the rent is due.

It is important to be certain that not only is your business well funded, but also that your domestic financial resources are adequate at the same time. So often a good business, possibly soundly funded at the outset, runs into difficulty later because the owners have had to draw out too much money from the business to enable them to meet domestic commitments.

If at the end of the exercise you are not totally sure that you have enough money to put both home and business on a sound footing, look for another business.

Assessing your own circumstances

Everybody's circumstances are different, so there is no magic formula. Nevertheless, the key issue is this. However carefully you may have investigated the business you eventually buy, you might find that there is not initially as much available cash to bring home as you had thought there would be.

There could be any number of reasons for this, not all bad ones. Maybe due to special circumstances there is a surge in trade and additional investment in stock is needed. Good news, but it might leave you short of cash for a while. On the other hand, you may take over at a bad time or at first you may not do as well as you could have done due to inexperience.

As already stated, it is vital to ensure that you are on a sound footing from day one. If you are short of financial resources right at the beginning things can only go from bad to worse, because somehow you will never recover, at least not for a long time. It is, therefore, essential to ensure that you have reserves in your domestic finances to enable you to survive in case of need without drawing on the business for a while.

How much do you need in reserve? Again, there is no hard and fast rule, but enough to enable at least three months' domestic spending to be covered without drawing on the business at all is probably a sensible amount. Obviously you hope not to need to draw on it, but it will give you great peace of mind to know that this cash reserve is there. If your spouse/partner is working, that income (if secure) may reduce the reserve you consider to be necessary.

Assessing the needs of the business

As you will be aware, some of the funding for the business can be arranged via debt, but some of your own resources will be required.

How to arrange finance in detail is covered in a later chapter, but at this stage you have to consider how much of your own money is likely to be needed.

When you come to look at a specific business you must consider the financial needs in great detail, especially if it is a seasonal business where the needs are likely to vary greatly throughout the year. In such cases a detailed cash flow projection will be required and, if you are not experienced in accounting matters, professional assistance will be necessary. However, at this stage just work out a rule of thumb to enable you to know the price of business you are able to consider. The detailed workings can be done later when you have a particular business in mind.

As a rule of thumb, assume that, if it is a leasehold business, you will need to find a third of the total costs of buying the business and the stock from your own resources. If it is a freehold business assume twenty per cent, because you can normally use the freehold as security for borrowing, thus enabling you to obtain a higher percentage by way of loan.

So how much can you afford?

Because of all the possible permutations in personal circumstances and business situations it is not possible to give fixed rules, only to indicate by way of example how to go about reaching a sensible conclusion.

Let's take a hypothetical example of the Smith family. The Smiths:

- Are interested in buying a leasehold post office.
- Have monthly expenditure of £2,000 and no other family income.
- Have a house worth £150,000 with a mortgage of £50,000.
- Have cash savings of £20,000.

To cover their family expenditure of £2,000 per month the Smiths will need to find a business that is making a profit of £24,000 after tax – i.e. about £30,000 before tax.

A post office making that much is likely to cost around 2.75 times the annual Post Office salary (see Appendix 3), which means that they can expect to pay about £85,000 plus stock (say, another £5,000), making a total investment of £90,000.

Can they afford it? Well, unfortunately not, unless the business includes accommodation and they can sell their house.

Firstly, they can only spend a maximum of £20,000 of their own money without re-mortgaging the house, which of course would increase domestic running costs. To contribute a third they would need £30,000.

Secondly, as you will discover when you read Chapter 6 on How to Assess What a Business is Worth, the profit on which the value of the business is calculated is the profit before any finance charges and repayments. In this example, if they invest £30,000 (by re-mortgaging the house) and borrow £60,000 on a business loan from the bank, they will have to pay the interest and repayment costs of the business loan, probably around £6,000 per annum, out of the £30,000 net income of the business, leaving them short on covering their domestic needs, which will have gone up slightly anyway as a result of the higher mortgage.

Thirdly, they will be left with absolutely no reserves.

Therefore, unless they can make savings at home, and re-mortgage by, say, £25,000 so that they have a cash reserve, they will need to think again.

What could they do instead? They can look for a post office with accommodation. Such a business may cost a little more, but would enable them to sell their house. This would put them in a totally different financial situation. They could then pay much more for a business, largely with cash from the sale of the house, and have a much better income. However, if they do not fancy living above the shop, or they see the house as a good long-term investment, they will have to look for something different altogether.

Let's look at a possible alternative. Because post offices are highly regarded they are relatively expensive compared with other businesses. If the Smiths were to consider, say, a sandwich bar, for example, they would only have to pay twice the annual net income. A sandwich bar making, say, £35,000 would typically cost around £70,000 with negligible stock. At that price they can just about make the maths work. Using our one third/two thirds rule, to buy the business they would need to invest £23,000 of their own funds and borrow £47,000 on a business loan. As they only have £20,000 in cash, they will need to re-mortgage the house to raise an additional £10,000 to give them the extra £3,000 needed for the purchase and leave them with a £7,000 cash reserve. The business should be able to cover the small additional mortgage cost involved.

In the Smiths' circumstances they have another option (which would not be available to people without a sizeable equity in their house). Provided they are prepared to take a little more risk by increasing their mortgage, they could use the equity in the house to support the purchase of a potentially more attractive business.

Suppose they added £40,000 to the mortgage, and put £10,000 in a savings account. They would then have put aside their reserve for a rainy day and, with the £20,000 already held in savings, they would now have £50,000 to put into a business as equity.

On the one third/two thirds basis as before, that would enable them to look at post office businesses costing around £150,000, say £140,000 plus stock. With post offices going for around 2.75 times earnings, for that price they ought to find a business making profits in the order of £51,000 per year.

The additional mortgage costs will be in the order of £250 per month (£3,000 per year), and the business loan cost (£100,000 over 10 years at, say, 10 per cent interest) would be around £16,000 per annum, so £51,000 less the £19,000 debt service would leave them with £32,000.

With the cash reserve in the bank, and £60,000 remaining equity in the house, they should not get into any financial situation they cannot handle and, provided that they check out the business thoroughly, they should not get into trouble anyway.

At this point a brief word of caution is, however, appropriate. If you are in the fortuitous position of the Smiths and have a sizeable equity in your house and you decide to borrow against it to fund a business purchase, please go to a mortgage lender. Do not fall for those advertisements on television for homeowner loans:

- Mortgages are generally much cheaper.
- Mortgage lenders are much more helpful in difficult times.

How much will different types of business cost?

When you look through the adverts you will see how much the kind of businesses you are interested in, and making the sort of income you need, appear to cost. Leasehold businesses generally sell for a multiple of the annual profit. This is referred to in business agents' parlance as 'Year's Purchase' (shortened to 'YP'). As we have already seen in this chapter, a café typically sells for twice the annual profit; in other words, on a YP of 2. The typical YPs listed in Appendix 3 will give you an initial idea of how much different types of the more common business sell for at the time of writing, but YPs can change over time so check with business transfer agents for the latest.

A rough and ready calculation as above will enable you to decide which types of business sectors are possibilities for you before you spend too much time looking. You will find it helpful to run it through a business transfer agent who will be able to give you lots of up-to-date advice. As stated elsewhere, although business transfer agents act for their vendors, good ones are more than happy to give general advice to potential buyers. It is in their best interests and that of their clients to do so, because they know that a lot of time can be wasted all round if they send purchasers to businesses that they have no chance of affording.

Chapter 5:

How to Find and Assess the Business

Finding the business

Finding the right business will probably take a good deal of time and research.

Newspapers and magazines

You will need to start with national or local newspapers, or trade magazines and papers. Nationals include:

- *Daltons Weekly.*
- *The Sunday Times* (mainly business-to-business).
- *The Daily Telegraph* (licensed trade, general, lifestyle).
- *The Financial Times* (generally more expensive businesses for corporate purchasers).
- Other nationals (franchise opportunities).

Local newspapers rarely carry many advertisements for businesses for sale, except for the larger regional papers such as the *Manchester Evening News*, *Yorkshire Post* and *South Wales Echo* which are well worth looking at.

Trade papers include:

- *Morning Advertiser* (mainly pubs).
- *Hairdressers' Journal.*
- *Hotel and Caterer* (hotels, guest houses, restaurants).
- *This Caring Business* (care homes).
- *The Subpostmaster.*

Daltons Weekly undoubtedly carries the widest selection of businesses for sale of any publication.

Use the Internet

Even if you do not have a computer yourself, find out how to use the Internet search engines and how to access the sites of the major publications, and go to a friend's or a library or an Internet café. It is not difficult and it will save you hours and hours.

By way of example, the leading search engine is Google. Try going to www.google.co.uk and in the search box type "UK businesses for sale". Within 30 seconds or so you will get pages of links to sites that sell businesses. When you see a reference that looks interesting, by clicking on the link on the screen you will be automatically transferred to the relevant web page. If you have an Internet connection at home you will find that the home page of your service provider will have a search facility. Many service providers use the leading search engines like Google to furnish their search facility anyway, so the result will be just as good as going direct to Google, Yahoo or whoever. The BBC website (www.bbc.co.uk) also has a very good search facility.

All the leading publications, including *Daltons Weekly*, are on the Internet, as are the leading business transfer agents. When you do your search, all these sites will be near the top of the list and, having clicked through to their sites, you can use search facilities on their sites to identify possible businesses of interest to you. For example, if you are looking for a wine shop, in the southeast of England, maximum price £50,000, you will be able to enter each of those criteria in boxes, click search and it will produce for you a list of all the businesses that meet those requirements. This is a much less arduous process than ploughing through papers and magazines.

In the case of business transfer agents, you will be able to register your details on their sites, giving a breakdown of your requirements, such as business type, maximum price, location, and so on, and you will be automatically notified when a suitable business becomes available.

Business transfer agents

Don't just rely on websites and publications. You should call the business transfer agents and discuss your ideas and aspirations with them. In many cases they have been selling businesses for many years and have a wealth of knowledge to offer.

Naturally there are good ones and bad ones and you will soon get to know which are which. Although they are acting for the seller, not you the buyer, they will be keen to advise you and help you find the right business if they think you are genuine. They know that trying to sell a business to someone totally unsuitable rarely works because there is almost always something that prevents the sale from going through – the buyer may realise it's not right, he asks his accountant who puts him off, or perhaps the bank won't put up the money. A lot of time can be wasted this way, so good agents will always try to put the right buyer with the right business if they can.

It is also in the best interests of the client. As a seller of a business you would want to feel that your business is being offered to the right people, and you would probably know from experience that the agents that are most successful in selling businesses are those that take the trouble to get to know about the potential buyers on their books. Therefore, the more the agent knows about you, the more helpful he can be.

Here is the best advice when dealing with business transfer agents:

ALWAYS TELL THE TRUTH

Experienced agents can tell someone who is exaggerating a mile off, and if they suspect that is what you are doing they will not be very helpful. They get many calls from timewasters and dreamers, and know that they cannot afford to spend time on either. Be prepared to offer detailed and truthful information about yourself and your circumstances openly and frankly. They will then not only trust you, but will also be in the best possible position to help you find the ideal opportunity.

GIVE THE AGENT YOUR WISH LIST

At the outset the agent will ask you for a run down on what you are looking for. Remember, you will need to be flexible to some extent – the exact fit is unlikely. However, as you specify what you are looking for, he will be able to offer you a considerable amount of general advice, and may help you fine-tune your thoughts.

At this point you will gain some indication as to how good this agent is. Try to find out, if you can, whether he charges the sellers an up-front fee, or whether he only charges when the business is sold. Unlike estate agents, it is not uncommon for a business transfer agent to charge a fee to put the business on the books. Some agents always charge an up-front fee, others only if they think the business will be difficult to sell. Some never charge an up-front fee. The latter only offer businesses that they feel a great deal of confidence about, and ideally these are the agents for you to deal with. Naturally, there will be some good businesses on the books of agents charging the up-front fee, and I am not suggesting ignoring them altogether, but obviously be a little more circumspect about believing everything they tell you.

IF HE'S GOOD, VISIT HIM

Most business transfer agents find themselves almost exclusively dealing with potential buyers over the telephone. If you want to stand out, make an appointment to see him. The personal contact always helps and, remember, when a little gem comes on the market you want to be the client who is first to see the details.

Now that you are on the agent's books (probably several agents), he will send you details of businesses he considers you might be interested to see.

Visiting potential businesses

Having now been given particulars of potential businesses, it is time to pay them a visit.

You can, of course, ask for an appointment to see the owner. However, if it is the sort of business with public access, it is generally a good idea to have a quick look around first, before making yourself known. Agents will normally disclose exact locations as long as you are clearly a genuine prospective purchaser.

If it's a pub, spend a while there as a customer and get the feel of the place. Is it busy? Are the loos clean and modern? Does the place need a lot of money to be spent on improvements? Do they obviously have a lot of happy regulars? Are they patronised by football hooligans or other undesirables? Do you like the bar staff?

If it's a convenience store, walk in as a customer and look round. Is it clean? Is it busy? Are there stale loaves and cheeses on the shelves?

What do you think of the general location?

You will be able to save yourself a lot of time if you can do this first. Save meetings for businesses that pass the test on this first look. However, in case this is a business you will wish to visit again, be careful not to be conspicuous to the staff. Under no circumstances ask to see the owner – any meeting must be arranged through the agent first.

Preparing to meet the owner

By this stage you have hopefully had a chance to have a quick look around, and no doubt a number of questions will already be in your mind. Make a list.

The agent will have sent you particulars. Having read these, no doubt you will have some general questions. Add them to your list.

The particulars also normally give some very brief information about the trade – turnover, gross profit and net profit. There should be figures for at least two, and preferably three, years, unless it's a newer business. At your first meeting you will not want to go into great analytical depth about the trading figures, but you will want to have a general chat about them. At this point, if you have no experience looking at profit & loss accounts, you should review the brief section on page 58 entitled Basics of the Balance Sheet and Profit & Loss Account, before proceeding further. At the first meeting you only need a superficial knowledge for general questions, which that section will give you.

Has the business been offered at a reasonable price? The next chapter, How to Assess What a Business is Worth, looks in detail at how to review the accounts in depth and reach a view on value. At this preliminary stage, however, you cannot go into that much detail, but you can sometimes work out a ballpark figure for a leasehold business by multiplying the weekly sales by a given number of weeks. In Appendix 3 there is a list of different business types where you can do that, with the relevant number of weeks to multiply by in the right-hand column. For example, the appendix indicates 30 weeks for a sandwich bar, so one that has sales of £2,000 per week is likely to be worth around £60,000.

It must be emphasised that the value this produces is very rough and ready, and assumes that profitability is at normal average levels for a business of that type. It can be used for picking out businesses that seem to be worth looking at more closely, and for preliminary discussions with the agent and vendor. However, you will need to do the proper valuation exercise covered in the next chapter before agreeing a price with the vendor. There could be many special reasons why any particular business is offered at a price widely different from this ballpark figure, but knowing the ballpark figure at least enables you to open a general discussion on how the vendor assessed the price he is asking for the business.

If it is a freehold business, then there is also the question of the property value to be considered and added to the ballpark figure.

Although you are not going to undertake a detailed examination of the trading records at this stage, the only way that you are going to be able subsequently to verify the accuracy of the trading information you are being given is by looking through the annual accounts and daily books kept by the business. The first key question, therefore, concerns the quality of the detailed accounting information you are going to receive in due course, and it is strongly recommended that you ascertain this before going much further. However attractive a business may seem at this stage, you are not going to buy it if you have no confidence in the truthfulness of the accounts.

All businesses have to submit annual accounts to the taxman, and this is normally done for the owner by an accountant or professional bookkeeper. Like all professionals, accountants and bookkeepers vary widely in competence and integrity. They have to include in the accounts a certificate of what they have carried out in preparing the accounts. If they have not been given all the reliable information that they would have liked, they should normally say so in the certificate. If the business is run through a limited company, the rules are laid down in the various Companies Acts and for larger companies a full audit is required. A good accountant will not put his name to accounts that he is not satisfied are genuinely accurate.

The annual accounts will have been prepared from the bank statements and bookkeeping records maintained by the business throughout the year. Obviously the annual accounts are more likely to be completely accurate if the daily records are well maintained than if paperwork is just tossed into a shoe box for the accountant to sort out later. It is also important to you that the bookkeeping records are good because annual accounts are likely to be at least ten months out of date, and possibly much more, and you will have to rely on the bookkeeping records to verify how trade has continued since the date of the last accounts.

Before you commit to buying the business, it is going to be essential to satisfy yourself that the trading information on which you are basing your decision to buy the business is accurate. You don't want to waste lots of time looking at potential businesses only to discover that the trading records are poor, so before going any further I suggest you ask the agent:

- How recent are the available annual accounts?
- Who prepared them?
- How good are the bookkeeping records?

Having decided to proceed to the next stage, prepare for the meeting with the owner.

A few key figures will have been included in the agent's particulars. Are sales going up year on year? If they have gone down, ask why? Have a look at the gross profit. This should be shown as a percentage of sales. You will find typical gross profits for some of the more common businesses in Appendix 2, but the agent will also be able to confirm this. Is it normal for that type of business? If not, ask why not. This question should be raised even if the gross profit is better than the norm, because you need to be certain that the unusually high sales prices can be maintained in the future.

Make a list of these general sorts of questions to ask the owner. It may sound pedantic to say 'make a list', but this is important for two reasons. Obviously you're bound to forget something if you don't but, equally, it is much harder for the seller to drive the conversation towards areas he wants to talk about, and away from those he wants to avoid, if you have a list you keep coming back to.

The other important issue you will need to discuss with the owner is the risks the business faces, and how well he has placed it, in so far as he can, to face those risks. The subject of risks was touched upon in the last chapter. However, now it is time for you to consider them specifically as regards the particular business you are looking at.

Is the business well placed to handle the risks it may face?

Some of the risks arise from external factors outside your direct control, and others from internal factors, which you may or may not be able to control. Prior to meeting with the owner, consider what risks could be involved, and add appropriate questions to your list. To assist you, listed below are some of the most common risks that could be relevant.

Location

In any type of business where the general public comes to you, the location is critical, but not always from the same point of view. Consider the location issues that apply in your case. Here are some examples to start you thinking.

1. Is visibility important? People will not come to your shop if they do not know it's there, or they just don't notice it. If you are a general retailer of some kind (flower shop, card shop, convenience store) you have to be very visible. When you have worked in retail, you quickly realise just how difficult it can be to get the public to see things. Often being just round the corner from the main road is enough to get overlooked. Check the footfall (footfall in this context being the term used by retailers to mean the volume of pedestrians walking past the front door).

2. Parking is likely to be important. People will not walk far these days, especially with bags to carry. If you are a post office it will be sufficient that you are very close to parking. If you are a television repair shop it will be important that people can stop right in front of or behind the shop.

3. Are there likely to be changes in planning that could adversely affect the business? It's important to consider this. Measures such as pedestrianisation, one-way systems, ring-roads, traffic-calming, etc., can devastate individual businesses. You will be able to judge from the general nature of the area whether such measures could be possible. If so, ask the owner, but also ask around in the neighbouring shops and bars (obviously be discreet about why you are asking), and approach the local planning department. A very successful privately-owned convenience store not far from London was sold a few years ago to one of the smaller chains. Two months after they had taken over they were banned from allowing cars to cross the pavement to park in front of the shop. This was because it was close to a pedestrian crossing and it had become very dangerous. The trade

dropped to a trickle, because the nearest car park was two hundred yards away across a busy road. Whereas being able to park outside had previously made it a very convenient shop, it was now considerably less convenient than other shops in the town. Needless to say, the previous owner had known this was coming, but obviously the chain did not carry out the right checks and suffered as a result.

Technology

This heading will not apply to the vast majority of businesses, but if your potential business relies heavily for its survival on technology in some way, there are a number of angles that could be relevant to consider.

OBSOLESCENCE

Is the technology used in your potential business likely to be phased out in favour of newer technology, or even completely replaced? If so, can the business adapt? For example, a television repair shop once dealt in valves, but without adapting to electronics skills, could not have survived to the present day. In the future, many technologies will be completely replaced at an ever-increasing pace.

MACHINERY

If your business depends on costly machinery, is it up-to-date? Small garages are a good example. These days more and more cars on the road rely on electronic diagnostics and tuning, and the small independent garage cannot undertake much of the repair work on these cars that it once was able to do.

Printing machinery, or machinery in small engineering works, can easily be out of date, possibly meaning that it is difficult, if not impossible, to produce work to a high enough specification for the modern client, or at a competitive price. If you are looking at this type of business you need specialist knowledge.

Competition

You will need to know what competition the business is facing now, and what you could face in the future. Consider competition in terms of:

- Existing local competitors.
- Potential for new competitors to come into the area.
- New alternative products.

Trends

Is the business a passing fad? Basically it is the entertainment type of businesses that are vulnerable here. Have karaoke machine sales peaked? How long will karaoke bars be popular? Be very wary of coming in at the end of a fad. Bars and pubs become the place in town to be seen, only to be overtaken by the new one that opens.

Internal risks

Internal risks are much more under your control, but you will want to discuss them with the current owner in order to assess the degree of risk, and how the risks are controlled by him.

Control of cash and stock

Obviously this is vital in all cash businesses with employees. Bars and cafés are particularly vulnerable, and breweries have gone to great expense to have sophisticated stock control systems to enable checks to be maintained.

Stock

Apart from the risk of theft already touched upon, there are a number of other stock risks that your business could face.

BUYING THE RIGHT STOCK

To what extent is it necessary to understand what your customers will buy? Is this the type of business where you could finish up with thousands of pounds of unsaleable stock because you bought the wrong items? A small newsagent's and tobacconist's shop may not be particularly problematic from this point of view, but greetings cards or gifts, and worse still, toys, could be a different matter. How does the current owner face this?

SOURCING STOCK WELL

Can the current owner introduce you to a range of suppliers who offer good products and good prices? We will deal with this again in Chapter 7, Verifying the Information You Have Been Given, when we cover the detailed verification process, because it is most important to satisfy yourself before proceeding whether the current owners have excellent supplier relationships. As a new owner of a business, in the early days you will rely on being introduced to good suppliers to get you going.

STOCK PRICE RISK

Is your business one where the value of stock can drop? A small computer shop, for example, would be very wary of carrying more stock than necessary, because today's highly desirable state-of-the-art processor chip will be overtaken (and therefore devalued) within weeks.

PERISHABLES

If your business stocks perishable items, how much is thrown away, and are the best measures taken to minimise loss? For example, a flower shop with a cold room will throw away fewer blooms than one without.

Reliance on larger customers/suppliers

Obviously a business that gets a high proportion of its business from a few large customers is inherently more risky than one with a broad spread of clientele.

The same can be said about suppliers. However, it is usually less of a worry to find alternative suppliers than it is to replace large customers who are lost.

Debtors

This risk has been left until last because it is not normally relevant to the vast majority of retail or catering types of businesses – usually it applies only to business-to-business type trades. If you are buying a cash business you need not worry about reading this section.

However, if the business sells on credit then you will have debtors. This is a subject dealt with in more detail elsewhere (Chapter 7, Verifying the Information You Have Been Given, Chapter 13, Paying for Stock and Debtors, and Chapter 10, How to Raise Debt and Equity Finance). However, debtors could be a critical aspect of the business's viability. In order to assess whether it is worth taking matters to the next stage, at this first meeting you will want to ask a few questions about how debtors affect the business and are controlled:

HOW MANY CUSTOMERS DOES THE BUSINESS HAVE, AND WHAT PROPORTION OF TRADE DO THE LARGEST REPRESENT?

In this type of business you are interested to know how well the business is spread across its customers. At this stage you should ask for a general indication of how many customers there are, and how much of the trade comes from the largest few. Clearly, a business with 100 roughly equal customers is less at risk than one where three customers provide 75 per cent of the business. In the latter case, what happens if one of the major customers goes elsewhere or goes bust?

HOW DO THEY DECIDE HOW MUCH CREDIT TO GIVE TO INDIVIDUAL CUSTOMERS?

Would your bank lend you £1million unsecured without making checks? There should at least be a system for taking references, and possibly credit insurance.

WHAT LENGTH OF CREDIT DO THEY OFFER?

Thirty or sixty days, and occasionally ninety, is normal.

WHAT LENGTH OF CREDIT DO THEY TAKE?

How good are the customers at paying on time, and what procedures are in place to chase-up late payers?

Meeting the owner

Remember, most owners will not have told their staff that they are selling, and are paranoid lest they find out. This confidentiality must be respected, so don't rush up to the counter and, clutching the agent's particulars in your hand, ask to see the owner, making it obvious why you are there. Be tactful!

The owner may be reluctant to talk when staff or customers may overhear. He may suggest that you pretend to be from the insurance company or something similar, but such covers usually will not work well, and anyway limit your ability to ask searching questions. Therefore it is best to resist this suggestion. If there is nowhere private on the premises, it is better to offer to visit after hours, or to go to a nearby café for a coffee or lunch. That way you will be able to have a much more relaxed and informative conversation.

Make it clear that you would like a general chat, but that you have a list of questions that you will wish to cover. Most business owners are keen to talk about their business, and why they think it's an exceptional opportunity that has probably been undervalued by the agent. You should be able to slip most of your questions into the general chat.

Look for any inconsistencies in what the owner says. Make a note for later of any points that strike you as important or in need of further investigation.

Why is he selling? Normally owners will say that it's due to ill health, or retirement, or to spend more time on the rest of their business empire. It's a question that people always feel they should ask. Intrinsically, it doesn't matter to you, as long as it's a good business opportunity at the right price. That is not to say you shouldn't ask, but sellers are not likely to tell you it's a decaying business that can't survive when Tesco's is open down the road! You may get a feeling that the truth isn't being told but, quite honestly, assess the opportunity on its own merits, based on detailed and careful research, and largely ignore the answer you are given.

More relevant questions are:

- How long has the business been on the market?
- Is anyone else interested?

Be very wary about businesses that have been on the market for a long time, or where there are no other interested parties. It may be that the business is a dud, or it could be that the owner is simply asking too much for it.

In the latter case you may wish to take the conversations

further of course. However, be patient about it, because it rarely pays to get into a price discussion at this early stage. All business transfer agents will tell you that business owners frequently convince themselves that their business is worth far more than it really is, and certainly far more than they would be willing to pay for it themselves if they had come along to buy it.

The problem is that vendors are usually very difficult to shake from this view, and they are certainly not going to change their mind in a first discussion.

If in all other respects the business looks appealing to you, raise the price issue with the agent when you go back to discuss your concerns with him. He will know the likelihood of the seller being willing to compromise. Obviously, you will not be able to take a final view on the value of the business until you have gone back for another meeting to go through the valuation and verification process described in the next chapter, How to Assess What a Business is Worth. However, if it is clear from these preliminary discussions that the price is far too high, there is no point in going through a more detailed and time-consuming exercise, or spending money on a professional valuer, if the agent indicates there is unlikely to be any substantive movement from the seller. In this case, move on. Do not be tempted to overpay.

After the first meeting

Having carefully prepared yourself beforehand, you will have probably managed to glean most of the information you need to judge whether or not it is worth taking further. However, when you sit down to think about it there are almost bound to be further questions that spring to mind, and possibly concerns that you would like to discuss in more detail. Speak to the agent – he will probably call you for your reactions anyway. A general chat with him will probably answer many of your concerns, and he can ask the seller for any additional information that you require that he does not have to hand.

Let's assume that at this point you have decided you like the business and, provided it checks out and the price is reasonable, you would like to proceed.

Before going further, you will need to have a feel for what a reasonable price for this business would be. The next chapter will give you the basic knowledge to be able to assess this, and at this stage you will need to call for the detailed accounts to enable you to undertake this exercise.

Obviously, once you have put a value on the business you will be in a position to make a verbal offer, subject to contract, and the negotiations can begin.

Chapter 6:

How to Assess What a Business is Worth

Evaluating a business is an art not a science. This is because there can be so many differing factors affecting the value of any particular business. Not least of the considerations is that any particular business can be worth more to one person than another.

Valuing a business is more complex than valuing a house. If you are valuing a standard house on an estate where all the properties are the same, the valuation process is very simple. However, if you have a unique house in an unusual location then the estate agent is likely to give you a bottom-line value, but indicate that if the right buyer comes along he could pay considerably more. The next valuer could suggest a completely different figure. No two businesses are identical, so, like the unique house, placing a value on a business is always an exercise specific to that particular business, and different people could place quite different values on the same business.

The following sections will take you through a step-by-step guide that will give you the basic knowledge to enable you to assess a business and value it from your perspective. In more complicated cases, with the knowledge you will gain here you will be confident to discuss the value of a business with a professional valuer and fully understand and assess what he is telling you.

Professional valuations

The first question to consider is: when should you obtain an independent professional valuation?

If you will need to obtain finance to fund your business acquisition, then it is highly likely that the lender will insist on one in any event.

It may well be a sensible precaution anyway, especially when undertaking a first-ever business purchase. It is certainly strongly recommended that you do so if the sums involved are substantial to you, or if you are in any doubt about the price you are being asked to pay.

Nevertheless, it is important to gain a reasonable understanding about how to go about valuing a business for yourself.

- In the first place, you will want to understand how the valuer has reached his conclusion, and be able to ask sensible questions of him.
- Secondly, valuations are generally rather expensive, and you cannot afford to have numerous businesses valued and end up not buying any of them.

You therefore need to enable yourself to work out at least a ball park value and reserve the independent valuation for businesses that you have thoroughly considered and valued and are keen to buy.

Reaching your own valuation

The starting point for evaluating a business is its annual accounts and trading records. You do not need to be an accountant, or even to have had any bookkeeping training, to follow the steps in this chapter, so do not be put off if you have no previous experience in looking at accounts.

Do not skip the rest and decide to leave it to an accountant to advise you. Accountants are, with exceptions, generally not the best people to give advice on business opportunities. If you are to proceed towards buying a business, it is important that you have the basic knowledge necessary to satisfy yourself that you are paying a reasonable price.

You do not need to understand the mechanics of the internal combustion engine to learn how to drive a car. Similarly, you do not need to understand accountancy, and how to prepare the final accounts, to be able to extract and assess the information you need from the balance sheet and profit & loss account.

For readers who have never seen a set of accounts before, the next section will give you a very simplistic look at these documents and enable you to understand the basic principles. Before continuing with the valuation process it is recommended that you take a look at it.

If you have seen accounts before you may wish to skip the next section.

Basics of the balance sheet and profit & loss account

The balance sheet

The balance sheet is a summary, as at a certain date, of the assets (what the business owns) and liabilities (what the business owes). The difference between the two is the owner's stake in the business (equity). The following is a very simple balance sheet:

Balance Sheet of Smith Supply Co as at 31st December [year]

	Assets (£)		Liabilities (£)
Van	10,000	Creditors	25,000
Stock	5,000	Tax	2,000
Debtors	15,000		
Cash/Bank	5,000	Equity	8,000
	£35,000		£35,000

In this example, the business has total assets of £35,000, consisting of a van valued at £10,000, stock which is worth £5,000, money owed to the business by its customers (called debtors) of £15,000, and cash in hand or in the bank account of £5,000.

The business owes its suppliers (called creditors) £25,000 and the tax man £2,000, making a total owed of £27,000. This means that if all the assets were realised and debts paid, there would be £8,000 left to share amongst the owners.

The balance sheet is thus a snapshot of the solvency or otherwise of the business at a specific moment in time (in this case after the end of trading on 31st December).

The profit & loss account

The profit & loss account is a summary of income and expenses incurred over a period of time ending on the date of the balance sheet. Usually, but not always, the period will be one year.

The following is a very simple example:

Smith Supply Co Profit & Loss Account for the period from 1st January [year] to 31st December [year]

		£	
Sales		200,000	(a)
Less Direct Expenses			
Cost of Stock		120,000	(b)
Gross Profit		80,000	(c)
Less General Expenses			
Wages	10,000		
Rent	17,000		
Power	5,000		
Bank charges	1,000		
Motor expenses	2,000		
		35,000	
Net Profit before Tax		45,000	
Tax		12,000	
Net Profit after Tax		33,000	

In this example, the business sales for the year were £200,000 (a). To achieve these sales it was necessary to buy in stock of £120,000, leaving a gross profit of £80,000 (c) to cover the general expenses. There are a few important percentages that are calculated from these figures and which will frequently arise in your discussions with business owners and business transfer agents.

To describe how the terms are generally used and how the various calculations work it is simplest first to use examples of individual transactions and then return to examine the Smith Supply Co accounts afterwards.

The transactions we will consider are a saucepan which cost your shop £6 to stock and was sold for £10, and cutlery which cost £8 and was also sold for £10.

The **mark-up** on the saucepan was £4. This is often expressed as a percentage of the cost of the item. In this example £4 as a percentage of £6 is 66.67 per cent. The mark-up on the cutlery was £2, a percentage of 25 per cent on the cost of £8.

The sale price less the cost is called the **gross profit** which in the case of the saucepan was £4. The gross profit is often expressed as a percentage of sales and referred to as the **gross**

profit margin. In the case of the saucepan the £4 gross profit amounts to a gross profit margin on sales of 40 per cent. The cutlery produced a gross profit of £2 on its sale price of £10, a gross profit margin of 20 per cent.

The two transactions in total have produced sales of £20, after costs of £14 leaving an overall gross profit of £6. The overall mark-up was therefore £6 on £14 costs (43 per cent), with the gross profit of £6 representing a 30 per cent gross profit margin on the total sales of £20.

In these examples you will notice that the amount of gross profit is always the same as the mark-up. However, this may not always be the case, because there could be other direct costs such as delivery, in which case the gross profit would be less than the mark-up on purchases by the amount of such costs.

Returning now to the Smith Supply Co Profit & Loss Account, the gross profit was £80,000, the average mark-up on purchases being 66 per cent (i.e. £80,000 as a percentage of £120,000 – **c** as a percentage of **b**). The gross profit margin on sales was 40 per cent (**c** as a percentage of **a**).

The gross profit margin is important, because the higher it is the more gross profit is available to cover the general expenses.

In this example, the business had general expenses of £35,000, leaving a net taxable profit of £45,000.

The reason that the direct expenses are normally shown separately from the general expenses is because they differ in one very important way. The direct expenses are directly related to sales, hence the name 'direct expenses'. The general expenses, on the other hand, are relatively fixed, whatever the level of sales. In the above example, had sales only been £100,000 rather than £200,000, then stock purchases would have only been £60,000 instead of £120,000. This would have left a gross profit of £40,000 to cover the general expenses of £35,000, and hence the net profit for the year would have been only £5,000.

If, on the other hand, sales had been £400,000, then after stock purchases of £240,000, the gross profit would have been £160,000, leaving a net profit of £125,000 after payment of the general expenses of £35,000.

Admittedly, a markedly higher or lower turnover in reality will often result in a certain increase or decrease in general expenses. Things like the use of the telephone, for example, or charges for cash being paid in over the counter at the bank, and probably labour costs, will increase to some extent if sales increase significantly. However, such expenses are not directly linked to sales volumes and some general expenses, such as rent, are usually unaffected by sales volumes. Consequently, overall changes in general expenses will normally be relatively minor in relation to the change in turnover.

Therefore, going back to the case of Smith Supply Co, we were able to calculate that if the turnover halves, all but £5,000 of the net profit is wiped out. On the other hand, net profit leaps dramatically if turnover doubles. This is typical of a business working on a relatively high mark-up on stock such as 66 per cent as in the case of Smith Supply Co.

But let's have a look at a business with a low mark-up, say 10 per cent, and see the difference. Let's assume Brown Trading has the same level of general expenses as Smith Supply Co (£35,000), and has a turnover of £1,100,000. The profit & loss account could be summarised as follows:

Brown Trading Co Profit & Loss Account for the period from 1st January [year] to 31st December [year]

		£
Sales		1,100,000
Less Direct Expenses		
Cost of Stock		1,000,000
Gross Profit		100,000
Less General Expenses		
Wages	10,000	
Rent	17,000	
Power	5,000	
Bank charges	1,000	
Motor expenses	2,000	
		35,000
Net Profit before Tax		65,000

With a mark-up of 10 per cent, sales of £1.1 million have produced a gross profit of £100,000, which yields a net profit of £65,000 before tax after paying the general expenses.

If sales halve to £550,000 the purchases of stock will halve to £500,000, resulting in a gross profit of £50,000 and a net profit after general expenses of £15,000. The net profit is considerably down, but not quite as dramatically as it was in the case of Smith Supply Co where the profit fell to £5,000 on halved sales.

Conversely, if Brown Trading's sales double, the net profit will increase from £65,000 to £165,000, an increase of 154 per cent compared to a 178 per cent increase in the case of Smith Supply Co if it doubles its sales. Therefore, we can conclude that a high mark-up business gains more relatively if sales increase than does a lower mark-up business, but equally is the more vulnerable if sales fall.

The other important consideration is the effect of failing to maintain the level of mark-up. Suppose that Brown Trading fails to maintain its 10 per cent and it drops by half to 5 per cent. On sales of £1.1 million the gross profit will be down from £100,000 to £52,381, leaving just £17,381 net profit after covering the general costs of £35,000. Conversely, if the mark-up at Smith Supply Co drops by 5 per cent, from 66 per cent to 61 per cent, the cost of stock for its turnover of £200,000 will only increase by £4,225 to £124,225. Thus gross profit will only fall by the same £4,225, leaving a more healthy £40,775 net profit after covering the general expenses.

What this shows us is that a high-turnover low mark-up business is much more vulnerable to pressures on its profit margins than a lower-turnover higher mark-up one.

Hopefully you will now understand the importance of the mark-up and gross profit to a business. The concept is basically very simple but, unless maths was one of your best subjects at school, may not be easily grasped at the first time of reading. As we will come back to the question of the gross profit margins and gross profits later when we look at the accounts in more detail, please do read this section over again until it is clear in your mind.

THE VALUATION PROCESS

When you buy a business there could be two elements to the purchase:

- Tangible assets.
- Goodwill.

Tangible assets may include long-term assets such as buildings (if owned), machinery, fittings and fixtures (display units in a shop, for example), and any other items of a capital nature.

Assets will also include short-term assets such as stock and debtors (money owed to the business by its customers).

Goodwill (often referred to by accountants and bankers as an 'intangible asset' since it has no physical being) is the sum of money you pay for the income-earning opportunity the business represents. For example, if you pay £15,000 for a mail order business which makes £10,000 profit in a year, and it is run from a room at home with only a telephone and no assets, you have bought the goodwill of the business for one and a half times its annual profit.

In broad terms, there are two approaches to valuation:

Investment method

The investment method involves calculating the proven level of profits, then, after taking into consideration how risky the business is, working out a capital sum you are prepared to pay in goodwill for that level of income – in other words, how much return do you want on your invested capital? In our example above, the decision was to pay £15,000 for a business earning £10,000 a year, a return of 66 per cent per annum on the £15,000 invested. This is the technique used to value most small leasehold businesses.

Assets method

Under this method you add up the value of the individual assets, including goodwill.

As you will see as you read on, the assets method is only used when the business has assets that have their own substantial value independent of the business – a warehouse, for example, or possibly a vehicle or a valuable piece of machinery that could be sold independently. Goodwill is one of the assets of the business, and is valued separately using the investment method. In the following sections we look at the valuation of tangible assets and goodwill in turn, and then see how we merge them to arrive at a final figure. We say 'merge' rather than 'combine', because the overall value we place on the business may well be an amount different from the sum of the parts.

TANGIBLE ASSETS

This section deals with the valuation of tangible assets. If your proposed business does not have an owned property or other assets with an independent value, but is run from rented premises, please read the section that deals with rented property on page 67, although you can skip the rest of this section and move on to the valuation of goodwill (page 71).

Long-term assets

It is highly likely that the business you are looking at will not include several of the types of asset discussed below. You do not need to read sections that are not relevant to you.

Motor vehicles

Obviously the easiest, since guides to values of vehicles are easily obtainable. The only word of caution is in relation to vehicles that have been adapted in any way. Adapting vehicles can adversely affect resale value. If vehicles are a significant element of the business purchase, then having a word with a local showroom, and possibly arranging vehicle inspections, may well be a wise precaution, even for standard unmodified vehicles.

It is also important to check whether vehicles are subject to finance agreements. It will either be necessary to ensure that the financing is cleared before completion or, if you are taking over the remaining outstanding finance, then the capital amount taken over should be deducted from the valuation of the vehicle(s).

Registers are kept of vehicle financing agreements so it will not be difficult for your solicitor to check the information you are given by the vendor when the time comes.

Furniture and equipment

The general rule is that items that do not have an independent resale value, such as furniture, shop fittings and so on, are normally ignored, as the payment for these is considered to be covered within the payment for goodwill.

Smaller items like calculators and computers are a matter of negotiation, and along with furniture and fittings, are often ignored unless the amounts are significant. Bear in mind that items such as these have very little resale value. Even a modern computer will lose half of its original value in a matter of just a few months.

Machinery

Again, small items that would have no significant value, such as hand tools, are regarded as having been included in the payment for goodwill, whereas larger and more valuable machinery, such as printing presses for example, that could be independently sold for a significant sum, are paid for in addition to goodwill.

In the latter case, unless it is machinery that you are very familiar with, it is essential to have a specialist's valuation report.

Specialists can advise not just on value, but also condition and obsolescence. It may be, for example, that the later generation of this type of machine is so much more cost-effective that you will not be able to compete for much longer unless you upgrade. In this case, not only is this machine probably worth no more than scrap value, but you will also need to budget for a brand-new replacement machine in the near future.

If you are faced with such expenditure in the near term, then you should consider this expenditure as part of the cost of the business, and in your calculations deduct it, or at least a part of it, from the value you ultimately place on the business.

Buildings

LEASED LONG-TERM

'Long-term', for present purposes, means longer than three to five years and where there is likely to be one or more rent reviews before the end of the lease.

At one time a long-term lease could be very valuable if it provided security of tenure for an attractive trading site. However, times have changed and business people are less and less keen to be committed to a long-term lease. If your prospective business is in a property that is subject to a long-term lease, then, if you are to proceed, you will have to accept an assignment over to you of that lease. However, there is very little likelihood that the lease has any value as such and, if the vendor or his agent is trying to convince you otherwise, you would be well advised to seek a property specialist's professional advice, especially if the sums are significant.

However, depending on the rent payable under the terms of the lease, there could be reasons to consider reducing the goodwill valuation (discussed in a later section), and so it is necessary to review the lease terms.

You should check, if at all possible, with other businesses in neighbouring units to compare rents to ensure that your unit is not unduly out of line with the market. It may seem impertinent, but most business people are more than open in complaining about the landlord and the rent! Obviously your vendor may not have told anybody that his business is up for sale, so be careful not to breach any confidentiality in making these enquiries. The commercial departments of local estate agents are also a very good source of information in this respect.

If you do discover that the rent is too high, then you can take the view that since the higher rent depresses the annual profit, and hence the goodwill value (discussed later), you will get the business at a price that takes the high rent into account. This could well be true, but remember that in almost all leases rents can only be reviewed upwards, and you will therefore be stuck with the unduly high rent until the market catches up, or to the end of the lease, whichever is earlier.

Check with the vendor about the date of the next rent review. It may be that there is a review in the very near future. If your rent is lagging well behind the market, you will find that there will be a substantial increase at the review date, and this will not be a case for simple negotiation. You will have to pay the higher rent unless an independent arbitrator rules otherwise. Future profits will obviously suffer, and this will have to be taken into account when assessing the goodwill value of the business (we will cover this later).

LEASED SHORT-TERM

'Short-term' in this context refers to leases of up to three, or possibly five, years, where the rent is fixed for the entire term. Usually a landlord would not be willing to commit to a fixed rental for longer than this.

For the purposes of valuing the business there are two issues:

- Potential changes in future rents.
- Security of tenure.

The issues relating to rents are exactly the same as discussed above for long-term leases. Even though it is a short-term lease, the landlord will expect a market rent, possibly a little more for the flexibility a short-term deal offers, so it is equally important as with longer-term leases to check the current level of rent against the market rate. If it is likely to rise significantly, you will need to allow for this in your goodwill valuation.

Whilst a short-term lease avoids long-term contractual commitments, the *quid quo pro* is that in a relatively short time you could be asked to leave. If that location is vital to your business, then you should consider whether to offer less for the goodwill of the business given this risk. Obviously, the risk is minimal if there are other equally good units close by, and this is the case on more and more high streets these days.

PROPERTY OWNED FREEHOLD OR LEASEHOLD

In most situations where a freehold property is involved, the property element of the overall price of the business is a very high proportion, possibly 85–90 per cent, so this aspect of the valuation process is very important in such cases.

Depending on the type of business, you can come very unstuck by overpaying for bricks and mortar.

In the housing market it is very difficult to come a cropper over the medium term. Even those people unfortunate enough to find themselves in negative equity in the early nineties were sitting on a nice equity just a few years later, if they were able to pay the mortgage and sit it out. However, in commercial property you can lose heavily if you are unwary.

Standard general business units such as lockup shops, warehouses, small modern industrial units, which are suitable for any number of differing trades, are easy to value, and the approach is similar to looking for a house. The local commercial estate agents will be able to advise you. Essentially, the value of the property will be a function of how much rent it could command if let, and current yields (the expected return on capital) for commercial/industrial premises of that type.

For example, suppose it is an 800 square feet unit, rents for similar premises in the same location are currently £20 per annum per square foot, and investors in the current market expect a 12 per cent income on their invested capital for an investment of that type. The calculation would go like this:

Annual rent income: £20 x 800 = £16,000

If £16,000 is to provide a 12 per cent return then the value is:

$$\frac{16,000 \times 100}{12} = £133,333$$

As already stated, you will have to rely on the local agents to supply you with current rents and yields, as these will differ from area to area. Since most agents still talk in terms of square feet rather than metres, our example reflects that.

There is one other factor to take into account with retail units only.

Visibility and public accessibility are paramount. Therefore a unit of say 1,000 square feet with a frontage onto the street of 40 feet in width must be more attractive than another of the same overall size but with a 20 feet frontage. To take this into account, for purposes of assessing rents, the space is divided into three zones:

Zone A is the area within 20 feet depth from the front;
Zone B is the next 20 feet back;
Zone C is the area further back or on higher or lower floors.

An agent will quote a Zone A rental, and when you do your sums you need to halve the area for Zone B and halve it again for Zone C. Assuming both properties are a standard rectangular shape, the calculations for the two above examples would be as follows:

Unit 1	40 ft frontage by 25 ft depth			
	Zone A 40 ft by 20 ft	=	800	
	Zone B 40 ft by 5 ft /2	=	100	
			900	sq ft
Unit 2	20 ft frontage by 50 ft depth			
	Zone A 20 ft by 20 ft	=	400	
	Zone B 20 ft by 20 ft /2	=	200	
	Zone C 10 ft by 20 ft /4	=	50	
			650	sq ft

Thus, when you speak to the local agents for rental rates, you ask for a Zone A rental figure and, to obtain the rental value, multiply it by 900 sq ft for Unit 1 and 650 sq ft in the case of Unit 2 rather than the physical size of 1000 sq ft. This zoning concept would not normally apply to other types of properties.

More specialised buildings, hotels, nursing homes, pubs and leisure centres, for example, are a different matter. It is very misleading when bankers and business valuers glibly talk about 'bricks and mortar values' on these more specialised business properties, without even mentioning the profits (or losses) in the underlying business carried on there.

In respect of hotels and care homes, agents and valuers often refer to a price per room (hotel) or bed (care home). These are guideline figures only and assume a normal level of occupancy at average charges. How can you say all two star hotels in London are worth the same per room? Naturally they are not, but if you are told, for example, that in Nottingham two star hotels change hands for about £65,000 per room, and you are looking at one which works out at £80,000 per room, then you have a starting point for a discussion. This is called the 'comparison method', and is used widely in these two industries. Perhaps your hotel is exceptionally well located and therefore maintains a much higher average occupancy rate than comparable hotels in the area. This should mean that the profits are better, and that is why it could be worth more than the average hotel.

The simple rule is this. If the building has specialised use only, then its value can only be regarded in relation to the profits it is capable of generating in that trade, at that location.

For example: let's consider a small hotel with, say, 20 rooms built 50 years ago on a busy 'A' road. Buildings insurance cover is £500,000 based on rebuilding costs. Occupancy was 70 per cent until last year when a new motorway was built nearby and the reduced passing traffic meant occupancy dropped to 35 per cent.

What is the building worth? The vendor points out that other hotels of a comparable standard in the area have been changing hands at £25,000 per room. Allowing for the cost of land, he asserts that the bricks and mortar valuation is therefore £600,000. After all, he says, you couldn't build it for less and property is an appreciating asset.

His problem is that he paid £750,000 for the business three years ago believing that at least £600,000 was covered by the bricks and mortar value of the property. As the previous owner was filling fourteen rooms a night it probably looked OK at the time, but now that he is only filling six to seven rooms per night he is not taking enough to cover interest payments on the mortgage. The problem for him is that neither could you. If you went to the bank they would probably say that the security for the loan is OK, but there is not enough income to cover loan servicing (interest and repayment), so with regret you would have to be turned down.

Therefore, you must look at the profitability of the underlying business to decide how much to pay, not just the apparent property value.

The one proviso to this is the possibility of alternative use. In our hotel example, it is possible that the building could be used for something other than a hotel. A nursing home might go well now that the road is quieter, for example. However, most specialised buildings would take a lot of work and cost to be adapted for an alternative use. A 50 bedroom hotel being converted into offices, for example, would need most of the bathrooms taken out and made good, and possibly a number of rooms knocked together to make large general office areas. The likely costs could be prohibitive, and would have to be deducted from any valuation on an alternative use basis.

In the final section of this chapter we will come back to the subject of how to value freehold businesses. In essence, the overall price paid for the business, including assets and goodwill, should not exceed a multiple of profits. Alternative uses for the property may give you a sense of ultimate security but, in the meanwhile, it is the current business that is going to have to pay the mortgage and other bills.

Short-term assets

As these items are easy to value – at cost in the case of readily saleable stock, and book value for all collectable debtors – there is no valuation technique as such. As both will be changing on a daily basis, and therefore it is not possible to calculate the final values until the day the business is handed over, stock and debtors are normally dealt with and paid for separately from the main purchase price. However, care has to be taken to ensure that too much is not paid, and this is covered separately in Chapter 13,

Paying for Stock and Debtors. It will be more important to read that chapter at a later stage rather than now.

GOODWILL

So far we have discussed how to value tangible items. In accounting terms goodwill is an intangible asset. Not only can you not touch it but, if you get the running of the business wrong, you can make it worthless. On the other hand, get it right and you can make your fortune!

Goodwill is the value placed on the business by virtue of its ability to generate profit. In essence, there are three steps in the valuation process for goodwill:

● Work out the annual profit you believe will be sustained in the future.
● Decide how many times the annual profit you are willing to pay.
● Multiply the one by the other.

Earlier in this chapter there was a section when we looked at the form a profit & loss account takes. Now we are going to take a more detailed example and see how we question the vendor, and make adjustments to the profit & loss account, to arrive at what we would consider to be a '**sustainable net profit**' for this business, based on the past trading records and other information. Therefore, if you still do not feel comfortable with the concept of the profit & loss account, gross profits and gross margins, please go back to page 58 and re-read that section before continuing.

Sustainable net profit

What is meant by sustainable? In deciding how much to pay for this business, we need to look at the past years to assess how much it is going to make for us in the future. To do that, we need to take out of the equation any exceptional items, or items that no longer apply. For example, suppose that last year the sales jumped by 40 per cent for a completely one-off reason, such as a large sporting event, for example, bringing thousands of visitors. Great, but this isn't going to help us next year, and we need to adjust the profits accordingly before concluding our calculations on value. A more mundane example might be the loss of the lottery terminal, which used to make £10,000 per year, but is not an available source of revenue for you in the future.

Equally, you must largely ignore, for valuation purposes at least, the vendor's statement that if he were staying he would diversify or expand into an additional business activity.

'If we were staying mate, we'd start doing baby clothes. There's no competition around here and you'll double your profits. That makes this business a terrific opportunity.'

This may be so, but whilst it may be a very good reason for deciding to buy this business rather than another one, it is not a reason for paying more for it. If he wants to cash in on the added value this new business activity might bring to his business, he should stay and do it himself and then sell it if he still wants to. If you do it, you should be the one to gain from the extra value put on the business as a result of your efforts and risk-taking, not him.

So, in summary, we are reviewing the records of the business, and other general information we have gathered, to assess the level of profit that is proven to be sustainable from ordinary activities, over the coming years, based on what has already been achieved. We will then determine how much we are prepared to pay for that earning opportunity.

This will involve taking a look at key items in the profit & loss account and, one by one, adjusting the amounts up or down as necessary to finish up with the final profit that is appropriate for valuation purposes. In the following paragraphs we look at all these key items in turn and discuss when and how adjustments need to be made to the figures.

Reviewing the accounts

To assist in presenting this topic we are using the ForgetMeNot Cards accounts as an example (as illustrated in the profit & loss account opposite), and will conclude by deciding a valuation for that business.

However, no set of accounts ever includes everything, and we will be discussing detailed issues that do not always apply in the case of ForgetMeNot Cards. In order to keep subjects in a logical order, all issues are discussed in sequence. When items discussed are relevant to ForgetMeNot Cards, a conclusion will be expressed at that point in the text.

ForgetMeNot Cards
Profit & Loss Account for the year ended 31st December

		Last Year		Two Years Ago	
		£		£	
Sales		169,293		128,473	
Cost of Sales					
Stock Purchases		86,214		57,511	
Gross Profit		**83,079**	(49%)	**70,962**	(55%)
General Expenses					
Wages	18,367			10,244	
Telephone	306			447	
Printing & Postage	832			434	
Advertising	-			15	
Motor Expenses	531			896	
Repairs & Renewals	219			543	
Insurance	956			629	
Accountancy	1,100			800	
Professional Fees	280			-	
Rent & Service Charge	23,938			18,870	
Business Rates & Water	9,795			8,210	
Light & Heat	801			800	
Bank Charges & Interest	68			52	
Depreciation					
Fixtures & Fittings	868			1,022	
Motor Vehicles	475			633	
Total General Expenses		58,536		43,595	
Net Profit Before Tax		**£24,543**		**£27,367**	

The ForgetMeNot Cards example is based on a real case (identity hidden, of course) so the exercise we are undertaking here is very realistic.

Remember the point of the exercise: to establish the level of sustainable future profit. What we are going to do now is to review every line of the profit & loss account to decide whether any adjustment is needed to the end profit figure shown in the accounts (in this case £24,543 in the last year), to produce the 'sustainable profit' figure we will be using for our valuation purposes.

As you will see, the ForgetMeNot Cards accounts show figures for two years. Two years' figures are adequate to make points that need to be made here. However, when you look at a business for real you should ideally review at least three years' figures (unless the business is not that old, of course). So if possible you should obtain the accounts for at least the previous year as well.

Having hopefully clarified the aims, at this point we can begin our review.

Sales

ForgetMeNot Cards sales in the last year were £169,293, a 32 per cent increase over the previous year (£128,473). In principle this sounds good, but a 32 per cent increase is rather a lot and needs explaining. With inflation running at 2 to 3 per cent an increase in sales of up to, say, 8 to 10 per cent would be healthy and not give rise to questions, but 32 per cent higher definitely needs an explanation. (Is it due to a one-off circumstance, for example, or is it sustainable?)

There are plenty of healthy explanations, such as:

● New product lines.
● Closure of local competitors.
● More customers due to improvement to nearby parking.

There could also be reasons that give rise to concerns on sustainability. For example, perhaps a local competitor has been closed for renovation, resulting in temporary increased trade which will disappear once it is open again.

If you feel that the volume of business is not going to be sustained, you will need to consider how profitable the business will be at the lower level of trade. When you need to make downward adjustments to sales, you also need to adjust stock purchases down at the same time. Let's look at an example of how to do it.

HOW TO ADJUST FOR LOWER SALES

Let's take the example of a greetings card and toy shop which makes a gross profit margin of 42 per cent. Turnover last year was £300,000, but for some reason you feel certain it will drop to £250,000 in the future. Last year's profit & loss account looked like this:

	£	
Sales	300,000	(100%)
Less Purchases	174,000	(58%)
Gross Profit	**126,000**	(42%)
General Expenses	85,000	
Net Profit	**41,000**	

If we want to see the effect of sales reducing to £250,000 we need also to reduce the purchases to 58 per cent of the lower turnover. The general expenses are not related to turnover and therefore are unaffected. The result is as follows:

	£	
Sales	250,000	(100%)
Less Purchases	145,000	(58%)
Gross Profit	**105,000**	(42%)
General Expenses	85,000	
Net Profit	**20,000**	

This again shows how vital the gross profit margin is. Sales have only dropped by 17 per cent but the final profit has halved.

Returning to ForgetMeNot Cards, we have been told the answer is that a second outlet has just been opened in a nearby town. The reason for the jump in sales is therefore clear and sustainable, so we do not consider it necessary to make any adjustments to the sales figure. However, since this second outlet is so new, and the final overall profit figure is down compared with last year (£24,543 compared to £27,367), obviously the new outlet traded at a loss in its first year. The jury is thus still out on whether it will become viable in the longer term. We will come back to this later when we discuss the final calculation of the sustainable profit.

Cost of sales – purchases

You will see from the accounts that last year sales were £169,293 and purchases £86,214, resulting in a gross profit of £83,079. The gross profit was 49 per cent of sales, compared with 55 per cent the previous year.

Usually the accounts do not show this percentage calculation, so you will need to make the calculation yourself (gross profit divided by sales times 100 for the non-mathematicians amongst us). However, many business transfer agents do include this percentage in the particulars they send out.

It is very important to look carefully at this percentage, and the changes year on year, because it demonstrates the trend in the mark-up the business is able to put on the items it stocks. It is this gross profit that will be available to cover general expenses and hopefully leave a final net profit for you.

These gross profit margins are pretty standard in any given trade. In Appendix 2 you will find a list of typical gross profit margins you can expect to see.

Because these margins are so typical, it is vital to check that the business you are reviewing seems normal and, if not, why not?

If the business covers two different sectors, say cards and toys, you will need to calculate a composite of the two for comparison to the accounts. To do this, you multiply the percentage of each product margin by its share of total turnover and then add the results together. For example:

Greetings Cards		=	70% of turnover		
			@ 50% gross profit margin		
Toys		=	30% of turnover		
			@ 25% gross profit margin		
	Cards		50 × .7	=	35
	Toys		25 × .3	=	7.5
			35 + 7.5	=	42.5%

So you would expect a business with a 70/30 mix of greetings cards and toys to have an overall gross profit margin in the order of 42.5 per cent. Obviously the figures are not exact. The norm for greetings cards is 50 per cent and, in the case of ForgetMeNot Cards, I would say that 49 per cent in the last year and 55 per cent in the previous year are within the range you would expect. In this case 5 per cent either side of the norm would not be unreasonable. However, you would expect a much smaller variance either side of the norm for lower margin items. Cigarettes and tobacco, for example, retail at margins of more like 9 per cent, and you would not expect more than 1 per cent or so either side of that.

If the margin is widely off the norm, investigate why with the vendor. There are endless possibilities, but some of the reasons could be:

If the margin is too high:

- Buying hooky stock!
- Sales mix in reality different from what you have been told.
- Poor record keeping.

If the margin is too low:

- Sales mix in reality different from what you have been told.
- Poor stock or cash control.
- Cash going straight into the owner's pocket.

Look at the trend of the gross profit margin over three years and, if it is dropping, investigate why. It could be a change in the sales mix. In the cards/toys example I gave above, if the toys became 40 per cent of sales instead of 30 per cent (and consequently cards 60 per cent), the overall margin would drop from 42.5 per cent to 40 per cent (try the calculation for yourself).

What adjustments to the profit & loss account are necessary?

If the margin is too low I would make no adjustment. Hopefully you can correct the problem, at least to an extent, and increase profitability.

If the margin is too high and no satisfactory explanation given, then you should recalculate the gross profit based on the normal margin, and reduce the final net profit accordingly. The following is an example of the calculation:

	Accounts as presented £		After adjustment £	
Sales	125,000		125,000	
Less				
Purchases	37,500 (30%)		56,250 (45%)	
Gross Profit	**87,500**	(70%)	**68,750**	(55%)
General Expenses	55,000		55,000	
Net Profit	**32,500**		**13,750**	

Snax Sandwich Bar shows a gross profit margin of 70 per cent, whereas the norm is 55 per cent.

This example demonstrates once again the vital importance of the gross profit margin.

In order to recalculate the margin to the 55 per cent norm we have increased purchases from 30 per cent of sales to 45 per cent.

The general expenses (wages, rent, light and heat, etc.) are the same, but by recalculating the gross profit based on norms, in this case 55 per cent, the effect on the final profit is dramatic, reducing it to less than half.

Going back to the case of ForgetMeNot Cards, the only question would be why it has gone down. Is it possible there has been a little bit of discounting in the new shop to encourage trade? Given that it remains within the normal range, we would not consider it to be necessary to adjust the accounts in this case.

General expenses

Having assessed the gross profit, you now need to go through the general expenses line by line to review what adjustments are needed to arrive at that 'sustainable future profit'.

Generally speaking, you need to go through each expense item looking for the unusual, or items of expenditure that are markedly changed from year to year, and seek an explanation.

It is obviously impossible to cover every single possibility here, but the items discussed below cover 90 per cent of the issues you are likely to need to consider. Not all are relevant in the case of ForgetMeNot Cards.

WAGES

It is very important to consider wages very carefully and to establish from the owner exactly what is included.

To take an example to illustrate the point, let's say you are looking at two convenience stores, both showing the same net profit of £50,000. Store A is run by the owner himself and four full-time staff. Store B is run by the owner, his wife, and two children, assisted by one full-time employee.

In the case of Store A the annual wage costs are shown as £40,000, whereas Store B shows £10,000. Would you want to pay the same price for each business?

Well, naturally not. The owner of Store B is lucky enough to have four family members to assist him, and the final net profit of £50,000 is the fruit of four people's labours. No doubt he is paying the family in cash. Store A, on the other hand, has made £50,000 after paying for four full-time employees. Store A is, therefore, inherently more profitable; after all, if he had had three family members to help him he could have saved three people's wages and shown a profit of £80,000 on a like-for-like basis with Store B.

The point here is that what we need to do is compare all businesses on a common basis so that we are comparing like for like – and the basis we use is the profit that would be made by a **single working owner**.

Therefore, when reviewing Store B we would need to adjust the accounts to reflect payment for the three additional family members at the going rate for the job. In our example, this is £10,000 per annum and accordingly Store B's wages need to be increased by £30,000, resulting in a reduced final profit of £20,000.

In some circumstances the opposite could be true – even the single working owner is drawing a wage. In that case, whatever he draws for himself should be added back – and the total wages for the year reduced accordingly, resulting in a corresponding increase in the final profit. This situation is most likely to arise if he is trading through a limited company.

DIRECTORS' FEES

Often when the business is run through a limited company, if the owner draws a salary it is shown in the profit & loss account under a separate heading 'Directors' Fees'. It is also not uncommon for other family members to be paid a fee, even though they may not work in the business.

If an amount for directors' fees appears in the list of expenses, it should be dealt with in exactly the same way as wages, so as to ensure the final profit is adjusted to reflect the profit to a single working owner, and therefore:

- It should be reduced to the extent that it relates to the principal working owner.
- It should also be reduced in respect of fees for any other directors who are not actually working in the business.
- Fees paid to second or subsequent directors for actually working in the business, if they form part of a normal level of wage for the job, should be left as they are. After all, if you buy the business you will need to pay someone to do these jobs.

PENSIONS

As with directors' fees, pension contributions should be added back to the extent that they apply to the principal working owner and other family members or investors. As such, they form part of the owner's drawings which will be available to you when you take over.

Until recently it has been fairly rare for a small business to offer a pension scheme to ordinary employees, and thus it has been fairly safe to assume that pension contributions were part of the owner's drawings. As such they could be added back to the profit. This is still the case in the vast majority of small businesses.

However, nowadays the law has changed and, depending on the size of the business (currently five or more employees), a pension scheme has to be offered to all employees. Obviously, any pension contributions made by the business for ordinary employees are an ongoing normal expense and cannot be added back to profits. Check for any anticipated future expenses in this regard.

In the case of ForgetMeNot Cards, only Wages appear in the accounts. There is a substantial jump in the last year to £18,367 from £10,244 in the previous year. We already know that a second outlet has been opened, and that is no doubt the reason why staff costs have risen. On enquiring, we have been told that since opening the second outlet the proprietor's wife has been assisting part-time without payment. The going rate to hire someone to replace her would be £5,000 per annum and, therefore, at the end of this exercise we will be adding this amount to the total wages and adjusting profits accordingly.

TELEPHONE, MOTOR EXPENSES

In the case of ForgetMeNot Cards these items are relatively small and would not really give rise to comment. In a card shop you would not expect the telephone bill to be very high, and use of a vehicle would be very limited. On the other hand, in a sandwich delivery business the van is essential and a higher cost would be expected.

However, you frequently see telephone or motor expenses of a personal nature put through the business to reduce tax or reclaim VAT, and people often get away with it. If the owner of Forget-MeNot Cards had a son in Australia, you could bet he would not telephone him from home!

You will need to review the expenses charged for these items and decide if they are reasonable in the light of the type of business.

The seller of your business might well have bought a car through the business, even though it may not in reality be bought primarily for business use. HM Revenue and Customs (who administer tax and VAT) have special schemes for the taxation of the private use of business cars, and so there would be nothing improper in this. What you need to consider is whether the expense charged is necessary for running the business or not. If not, you can regard it as personal drawings by the proprietor and add it back into profits.

For example, suppose for a moment, the proprietor of Forget-MeNot Cards had leased a car through the business, then the following items might have appeared amongst the general expenses:

Lease of motor vehicle	£1,600
Motor expenses	£800

As a card shop it might be necessary to do a little running around, but not enough to warrant charging the business £2,400. After discussion with the seller as to how much running around he does, you might conclude that 500 miles per year are involved, in which case the true cost incurred as a result of the business could be assessed at, say, £400. In this case, you would regard £2,000 as personal drawings from the business, decrease expenses accordingly and, as a result, profits will increase correspondingly.

You will need to take similar steps in respect of telephone charges.

Of course, no such undue charges appear in the case of Forget-MeNot Cards, so in our exercise, as already stated, we will not need to be making any adjustments to the profits for these items.

REPAIRS AND RENEWALS

'Repairs and Renewals' should be for small running repairs and renewals of smaller items of equipment. Major refurbishments and purchases of higher cost items of equipment, which are in the nature of investment in items that will serve the business over a number of years, should be regarded as capital expenditure, and not included in the profit & loss account (see Depreciation on page 86).

Business owners often, however, include capital items under this heading in the hope that the taxman will let them claim tax relief, so you will need to examine what has been included under this heading to ensure that you use a realistic annual figure in the valuation.

When you review the accounts of your target business, you will need to assess what a reasonable average annual cost of such items would be, and adjust the figure in the accounts accordingly. Obviously this will vary enormously from business to business, and you will have to assess it on a common-sense basis in each case. All we can do here is use ForgetMeNot Cards by way of illustration.

In the case of ForgetMeNot Cards, at £219 and £543 in the past two years respectively, clearly no larger items have been included.

However, let's suppose just for a moment that last year the figure under this heading had been £4,500. Common sense suggests it is highly unlikely that a small card shop would spend that much on general maintenance items such as repairs, renewal of the vacuum cleaner or kettle, etc., so enquiry would need to be made to ascertain what has been included in this figure. Being a card shop, the most likely answer would be either new fittings (card racks, for example) or redecoration of the shop. As it happens, the taxman would probably be happy for the redecoration to be charged to profits in one year like this, but would not be happy about the racks, which he would regard as being of a capital nature.

In either case, it is not realistic for you to assume that this level of expenditure will occur every year, because it won't, and the effect of including it would be to underestimate the general profitability of the business. If the answer we received was 'card racks', then the item should be deducted altogether, as it is capital equipment and we will discuss this later under Depreciation. If the answer was 'cost of redecoration', which is obviously in the nature of repair or renewal/maintenance, then it should be dealt with here. However, in order to come up with a reasonable figure for valuation purposes you would need to spread such expenditure over the number of years of its useful life to calculate the average annual expenditure. Then you adjust the amount charged to the profit & loss account each year to reflect such annual average expense.

Going back to the actual accounts of ForgetMeNot Cards, there is no reason to doubt that £219 was the actual expenditure last year. However, it is far too low for the purposes of valuation. It is a reasonable figure for the little everyday items, but being a card shop it will need to look smart to maintain its business and will have to be redecorated, say, every five years or so. If we guess that decorating would cost around £2,500, then we need to increase the figure of £219 in the accounts by £500, to £719 to produce the realistic annual average we are seeking.

INSURANCES

All businesses require business insurances of one sort or another, but they vary considerably from one business to another. You will need to approach a broker that specialises in business insurance to obtain an indication of the likely costs in your particular case and, naturally, adjust the figure in the accounts accordingly if the amount appearing under this heading is widely different.

ACCOUNTANCY

If the business has employee(s) running the day-to-day bookkeeping, their costs will be included under Wages. Accountancy will include the cost of employing external accountants to prepare the final accounts and tax returns for you, and for doing any bookkeeping if it is not done internally. You may wish to compare the figure in the accounts with an estimate from your own accountant to see if it is significantly different. Adjust the accounts if appropriate.

PROFESSIONAL FEES

These often include lawyers' and/or surveyors' fees and are often one-off fees that do not occur every year and thus distort the picture of overall profitability.

For example, suppose that in the year covered by the accounts you are reviewing, the lease came up for renewal. Negotiations would have to take place between the vendor and the landlord on the renewal terms – both in respect of the general terms of the lease and the level of the rent. Solicitors would advise on the former and commercial agents/surveyors on the latter. As with the redecoration costs we discussed under Repairs and Renewals, these costs may have arisen in the year covered by the accounts you are looking at, but will not recur every year. Therefore, you cannot reasonably assess profitability on the basis that this is an annual cost, so divide these types of cost by the number of years they cover: if, for example, rent reviews are every five years then adjust the accounts to reflect one fifth of the cost per year.

There are many other reasons why expenses may appear under this heading, which is a good example of why you should look at several years' accounts. If fees appear year after year you need to know why. If every year fees are being spent on recovering money from debtors, for example, is the customer base sound? Perhaps your interest in the business should end here.

RENT AND SERVICE CHARGE

Rent is self-explanatory. Service charge usually applies where a business is located in a retail or business centre where a charge is made for management services.

We have already discussed leases earlier in this chapter and the need to ensure that costs to the business are not about to escalate.

Check with the seller, if you have not done so already, when the lease comes up for renewal or rent review. If it is within the next two years, adjust the accounts to reflect any increase your enquiries have revealed may transpire.

To be fair, with the general demise of the high street, this is less of a problem than it used to be in respect of retail units, but is still particularly important to consider for industrial or warehouse units.

GENERAL AND WATER RATES

The only comment to be made here is that if the rateable value of the premises is considerably more than what is being paid in rent, beware the next rent review!

BANK CHARGES

This heading can cover two items that are very different:

- Charges for running the account.
- Interest charges.

It's virtually impossible to run a business these days without a bank account, and charges will be made by the banks for this service. There are no comments to make at this point in terms of general commission charges (except don't you wish you owned a bank!).

Interest charges are another matter. If the current owner has borrowed money to finance the original purchase of the business or the acquisition of additional assets (a computerised stock system, for example), the interest charges will appear in the profit & loss account. Businesses also borrow on overdraft for working capital. All these interest charges should be removed from the profit & loss for valuation purposes.

Why? Well, because we are trying to decide how much to invest to acquire this business opportunity – how it is funded is irrelevant. The best way to illustrate the reason is by way of an example. Let's consider a business making £30,000 profit per annum with no interest charges. If for that business a 30 per cent return on investment is right then the price agreed will be £100,000. For simplicity, let's also assume that the purchaser makes exactly the same £30,000 profit in his first year.

- If Purchaser A pays entirely from personal cash, he will show a **profit of £30,000** in the profit & loss account.
- Purchaser B has £50,000 cash and takes a bank loan of £50,000 for the balance, incurring an interest charge of £5,000. His profit & loss account, after deducting the interest charges, will show a **profit of £25,000**.
- Purchaser C has £25,000 in cash and borrows £75,000. His profit & loss account, after deducting interest of £7,500 will show a **profit of £22,500**.

Each purchaser has shown a different final net profit in his accounts, but each has invested the same total sum of £100,000. In effect, they have all made a profit of £30,000, it's just that Purchaser B and Purchaser C have had to share that profit with the bank. The permutations on funding the acquisition are endless and irrelevant. We can only assess the business on the amount it makes for the funds invested and leave the division of the profit amongst the owners and funding providers out of the equation. In this example, £30,000 is accordingly the only profit figure we can base our decision on.

The problem often faced when reviewing the accounts is that bank interest and commission charges are frequently combined under one heading and the vendor will need to be asked to supply the split.

In the case of ForgetMeNot Cards, no interest has been deducted and, therefore, there is nothing to be added back into profits.

DEPRECIATION

This is the final item under general expenses that needs discussion.

Depreciation is the charge made to the accounts to write-off the cost of capital items (assets) over their useful lives. It would be typical to write-off equipment and furnishings over five years. The Institute of Chartered Accountants in England and Wales, and their equivalents elsewhere, have accounting rules that their members are obliged to follow in preparing the final accounts for you. Whilst these rules are designed to make the accounts as accurate and clear as possible in an accountant's eyes, they do not always achieve this objective for us ordinary mortals. Usually the depreciation charged is a reflection of what can be agreed with the taxman rather than what is realistic in practice.

By way of example, if you buy a desk for £500 you will probably be allowed to write it off over five years – in other words deduct £100 per annum from the profits over each of the next five years. That will naturally reduce tax, but will you really throw the desk out after five years and buy another one? Perhaps you will, but only if you fancy a new one. It is far more likely that you will still be using that desk in fifteen years' time, so it can hardly be said that it has cost £100 per year.

If the seller of the business renewed all the fixtures and fittings in the last few years you will probably find some hefty depreciation charges to the accounts as the accountants write it off over five years. Depreciation is, therefore, something that always needs looking at carefully from a business valuation point of view.

You need to consider what has been covered by the depreciation charge and whether it is realistic. Franking machines last more or less for ever, well-maintained card racks will look OK for ten years, whilst cars lose half their value in less than three years. Consider the assets involved, and calculate a reasonable depreciation charge based on writing-off the assets over their realistic useful lives.

The converse can be true. If the fittings in the shop have been there for years, they are probably looking tired and will need to be replaced. In that case, little or no depreciation will have been charged to the accounts. Calculate what you are going to need to spend in upgrading and divide that expenditure by the useful life. Deduct the resulting figure from the final profit as a depreciation charge.

As with other headings we have discussed under general expenses, deduct any amounts charged that relate to personal drawings. In the case of ForgetMeNot Cards we have already decided that the limited use of a vehicle is not sufficient to regard it as reasonable to charge all the costs of a vehicle to the business. In similar situations, any depreciation of the motor vehicle should be deducted from the expenses.

Finally, you will sometimes see an allied item called 'amortisation of goodwill'. If this item appears in the accounts, remove it. Amortisation is the equivalent of depreciation for intangible assets such as licences or goodwill. If you have bought a licence to run the National Lottery for five years, then it is reasonable to write-off the cost over five years because you may be thrown out after five years and, even if not, you will be expected to pay another premium to be allowed to continue for the next five years.

But if you pay £100,000 for the goodwill of a business, you are hoping to improve the business and increase the goodwill value. There is no finite lifetime for the business, so the concept of writing-off the amount paid for goodwill is an accountant's nonsense. As a matter of interest, in support of this argument, you would find it next to impossible to get the tax inspector to accept it as a legitimate business expense, deductible for tax purposes!

FINAL CHECK

In the preceding paragraphs we have considered just about all the items that will always need to be looked at. However, we should take a final look through all the general expenses to find any unusual items or any expenses that have changed dramatically from one year to the next.

Consider each expense, line by line, and figure out whether on a common-sense basis it seems logical for the type of business and level of trade. If you are in doubt, ask the vendor how that level of expenditure arose, especially if it seems on the low side.

In the case of ForgetMeNot Cards the item that stands out in this respect is Printing and Postage. In the first year the charge to profits was £434, whilst in the following year this jumped to £832. Think about your local card shop. How, in normal circumstances do you think they might spend over £800 under this heading? Why in the case of ForgetMeNot Cards did the cost double? A card shop and, in fact, most small retail businesses for that matter, would only have a very low expenditure on postage, and in many cases virtually no printing costs, possibly none at all. The most likely explanation in the case of ForgetMeNot Cards would be promotional leaflets and/or mail shots for the new shop. This would not be a recurring item in a business relying entirely on passing trade and therefore we should reduce the charge in that last year. In all likelihood, the cost of these items in a normal year for a small card shop would be unlikely to be more than £20 per month, so even the first year seems on the high side. However, to be conservative let's reduce the figure in the last year to about the same level as in the previous year – i.e. reduce it by say £400 – and leave the previous year as it is.

We have now reviewed all the key expense items that need to be reviewed, and can move on to calculating the revised profit for valuation purposes.

Calculating the adjusted profit

Now that we have been through all the profit & loss categories, let's recap the adjustments we decided to make to our example case ForgetMeNot Cards. There were four:

- Increase Wages in the last year by £5,000 in respect of the part-time work of the owner's wife.
- Increase Repairs & Renewals by £500.
- Decrease Depreciation to remove motor vehicles: £475 last year and £633 the previous year.
- Reduce Postage & Printing by £400 in the last year.

So let's now recalculate the net profit in the two years.

		Last Year	Two Years Ago
		£	£
Net Profit per accounts		**24,543**	**27,367**
Increase Wages cost	-5,000		-
Increase Repairs & Renewals	-500		-500
Reduce Printing & Postage	+400		-
Decrease Depreciation	+475		+633
Net Adjustment		**-4,625**	**+133**
Adjusted Profit		**19,918**	**27,500**

Now we have reached the time for a decision. Based on the adjusted profits above, what are we going to regard as the sustainable profit for the purpose of calculating what value we will put on the business?

In the next section we will take the ForgetMeNot Cards case as an example for valuing the goodwill value of a leasehold business. In the section after that, we will discuss the differences for freehold businesses.

CALCULATING THE VALUE OF GOODWILL

When we discussed our preliminary assessment of businesses for which we have been sent details, mention was made of the rule-of-thumb guide using a multiple of week's sales. That produces a rough guide but at this stage is nowhere near reliable enough.

The value of goodwill depends on three main factors:

- Degree of risk.
- Hours of work.
- Profit.

Degree of risk

The degree of risk is reflected in the valuation by how many times the annual adjusted profit you are prepared to pay for the business (often referred to as Year's Purchase or YP for short).

In Appendix 3 there is a list of typical YPs for the more common types of businesses. Let's take a couple of examples using the relevant YP from the list:

| Off-licence making £20,000 p.a. | YP 2.0 | Value £40,000 |
| Newsagent making £20,000 p.a. | YP 2.5 | Value £50,000 |

As you will see, although they are currently making the same profit, the off-licence is generally considered slightly more risky than the newsagent; consequently it is valued lower at only twice the annual adjusted earnings.

In general, this is probably fair comment. Newsagents usually carry a wider range of product groups, and have added stability from the paper rounds. Off-licences arguably face stiffer competition from the supermarkets (who unlike the newsagents don't deliver papers), and their trade is more seasonal.

You will also notice on the list that a café or sandwich bar would be valued at between 2 and 2.5 YP, whereas a licensed restaurant would rate a lower YP of 1.5 to 2. Again, in general terms this must be right. It is certainly more risky to run a £30 per head *à la carte* restaurant than a *greasy spoon*. But some licensed restaurants would be inherently more risky than others (a balti is less risky compared with an exclusive French restaurant, for example) and hence the range of YPs under some of the headings.

Hours of work

The other factor that can affect YP is unsocial hours. A café which is only open at lunchtime five days a week would certainly sell on a higher YP than one that has to open six days a week, evenings as well, to make the same money.

The YPs in Appendix 3 are indicative, and you might well find a business on the market on a higher or lower YP than on our list. This may be because the owner is looking for an unrealistic price, or perhaps the business transfer agent will justify it to you in the light of special circumstances. However, the YPs on our list are the current norm and should be used as the basis for your initial valuation calculations.

Appendix 3 includes most of the usual businesses that change hands. But what if your target business is not on the list? In that case, you will have to do some investigation work which is covered in the appendix.

Profit

As we have already discussed, the profit used in the calculation is the profit we have determined to be proven to be sustainable in the future.

What we need to do now is to discuss how we decide what we consider the proven sustainable net profit to be.

With most businesses, unless something is awry, or something dramatic has happened, the turnover and profits do not move significantly from year to year and, having made the adjustments, it is pretty clear what level of profit the business will sustain. Let's take an off-licence, for example, and say that your adjusted profits for the last three years are £45,000, £48,000 and £50,000 (most recent year).

So, in a simple situation like this it is just a case of multiplying the adjusted profit by the YP.

Some valuers would take the average profit in the last two years, some the average of the last three. In this example that would be £49,000 or £47,667 respectively. On a YP of 2 this produces a valuation of £98,000 or £95,334. However, it would not be unreasonable to suggest that the profits indicate a pretty stable business and £50,000 would be the minimum it will make in the future, in which case the value would be £100,000. It won't actually make a very significant difference which of the figures you use in this case, and it would be like this in many of the businesses you look at. In this example you would probably make an offer of £95,000 and be prepared to increase it by up to £5,000.

The most important factor is that you have made all the necessary adjustments to the accounts to arrive at the appropriate profit figures to base the valuation on and have factored in for any foreseeable downside.

What if sustainable profit is not so clear-cut?

In the example of the off-licence above, the final calculation is pretty straightforward. This will probably be the case in the vast majority of small businesses you will look at.

However, sometimes there could be factors that are not so clear-cut. Obviously, it is not possible to cover every possibility, but what we can do is take an example to show the general approach.

Let's continue by valuing ForgetMeNot Cards.

You will recall that our adjusted profit last year was £19,918, despite higher sales. This was down from £27,500 in the previous year.

In the case of ForgetMeNot Cards we do have a special factor that has meant a sharp reduction in profitability – a new unit has been opened and in its first year has sustained a loss. So what profit shall we base our valuation on?

In Chapter 5, How to Find and Assess the Business, the point was made that if the current owner believes something new will increase profitability then he should stay and prove it if he wants to benefit from the uplift in the value of his business. On that basis you might take the view that £19,918 is the figure, and it is difficult to argue against that position. However, how keen are you to buy the business? Perhaps having seen the new unit you are totally convinced it will be successful. We know that the first unit is capable of making £27,500, because it did so in the previous year, so in that case there is an argument for assuming break-even for the new unit and taking £27,500 as a reasonable profit to use as the basis for the valuation.

The final decision in a situation like this is down to you. Let's assume that you do like the new location, and you are keen to acquire the business for its growth potential. Businesses with real potential like this are a relatively rare bird and worth paying that little extra for. In these circumstances you could certainly take £27,500 as a basis and might even go to £30,000, on account of the fact that the new unit has been established and is not just an idea in the mind of the current owner, who has been able to demonstrate that its sales have been steadily growing during the short period it has been open.

Let's look at a matrix of possibilities.

		YP	
Profit	**2.25**	**2.5**	**2.75**
19,918	44,815	49,795	54,775
27,500	61,875	68,750	75,625
30,000	67,500	75,000	82,500
35,000	78,750	87,500	96,250

The standard YP for a card shop in accordance with our list in Appendix 3 is 2.5 and, as discussed above, based on the information we have gleaned or assumed, it would be reasonable to use

£27,500 as the profit figure in our calculations. On that basis you might hope to get the business for £68,750.

If you were really excited about the potential of the new unit, you might feel willing to use £30,000 as the profit figure and go to £75,000 – after all, the unit is trading, the work of setting it up has been done and the furnishing of the premises carried out. Looked at another way, if the owner said that with the potential the business offers you should be prepared to pay a higher YP, then £27,500 profit on a 2.75 YP produces as near as makes no difference the same valuation (£75,625).

In all probability, the business would have been offered for sale at around £87,500, the owner believing that adjusted profits will be at least £35,000 now the new unit is on its feet. If the owner stayed and made £35,000 next year he could certainly justify his price. However, as stated previously, since he is selling before proving the potential he must expect to sell for somewhat less. A price of around £75,000 would seem a reasonable compromise.

If, on the other hand, you were not convinced about the new unit, then you could offer to buy just the first unit. In that case you would use the normal 2.5 YP on the £27,500 profit (the profit it was making without the second unit losses), and negotiate up to £68,750. If the owner insisted on selling both, then you would most likely walk away, and should. If not, you would have to use the profit figure inclusive of the losses (£19,918), and around £50,000 would have to be your top price. On that basis it would obviously not be a realistic basis for agreement.

These are all ifs, buts and maybes. However, hopefully they give you a feel as to how to approach working out a reasonable price to pay when the sustainable profit is not so clear-cut. If you find yourself in this situation, using the knowledge you have gleaned from reading this chapter debate it with the business transfer agent until you are clear in your mind as to what your maximum price is.

What if the business is making losses?

Occasionally businesses that are losing money, but which are thought to have good potential, are offered for sale. Dixons sold Freeserve without ever making a profit! If you are considering such a business, how should you approach placing a value on it?

The first thing to be said is be very careful, especially if you are a first-time business buyer. In projecting future profits you are moving into the largely unknown, and this is usually best left to the more experienced businessperson.

Whilst financing is covered elsewhere in this book, it is worth mentioning here that banks and other business lenders are very reluctant to lend for the acquisition of loss-making businesses, particularly when the purchaser is inexperienced. They would certainly be looking for solid security, which most likely would have to come from personal assets, but it is more likely that you will have to put up all the funds yourself.

Generally speaking, it is not worth even looking at retail or café businesses that are making losses. If the current passing trade does not adequately support the shop or café, it will be impossible to be assured of what effects any change in parking or road layout due in the future may have on the public's buying habits. It is remarkably difficult to get your business noticed by the public if it isn't already, and advertising is expensive and rarely works in such situations. Similarly, the fortunes for restaurants are almost impossible to predict.

However, possibly you are looking at something different, like a mail order business, for example, which is growing but has not yet reached break-even and which you feel has great potential. In such cases, in addition to the accounts to date, the vendor must provide you with some projections for the next two or three years. You will then be able to assess how the business will progress, how much it needs to expand to move into a worthwhile profit, and how long that will take.

Having read the earlier parts of this chapter you will know how to look through the accounts and what questions to ask. Make the same adjustments to the figures as we have already discussed and work out what you think the adjusted profit will be for the next two years. You cannot look beyond that or take any projections beyond that into consideration when agreeing a price. If you are not convinced that it will make money in less than two years it is worthless.

Because the profits you are assuming are not proven you cannot apply a full YP as in the case of a currently profitable business. You will want to negotiate a price that represents a substantial discount below what you would have paid had the profits already been achieved. As to how much of a discount, it is impossible to generalise. Let's take an example. Let's assume we are looking at a business that lost £20,000 in its first year, is currently losing £10,000 per annum, and you believe will make a profit of £10,000 profit in the next year and £20,000 thereafter. We will assume the YP for the type of business is 2. How much should you pay if you are convinced it is a good long-term opportunity?

The vendor is going to claim that as the racing certainty is that you will be making £20,000 in less than two years, and much more as time goes on, you should be prepared to pay a YP of 2 on £20,000 – a price of £40,000. He might concede the YP could be worked out on the average profit projected for the next two years (£15,000) and accordingly suggest a price of £30,000.

If you could be assured of making the projected profits, a price of £30,000 would be fair. However, in view of the current losses, a price of around £15,000 would be more appropriate. Should the vendor reject this and you are keen not to lose the business, there is another approach – deferred consideration. You could offer him £10,000 now, with a further £10,000 in each of the next two years if the projected sales are met. This would need a special contract to be drawn up by legal advisors, and an independent audit of the accounts, but would be a better deal all round. The vendor is convinced the potential is there and will receive more for the business than you are prepared to risk up front, whilst you risk less outlay whilst there is uncertainty. Obviously there are endless permutations on these lines, but hopefully this will give a few ideas on how such a situation can be approached.

One final word of caution must be made. Buying a business that does not have proven profitability is high risk. Even in experienced hands predictions of future business potential are fraught with scope for error. If the sums are substantial do take quality professional advice.

CALCULATING VALUE – BUSINESSES WITH BOTH VALUABLE ASSETS AND GOODWILL

So far in this chapter we have only looked at valuing businesses that do not have valuable assets other than their goodwill. We are now going to look at how to value a business that has valuable tangible assets as well.

The general approach is as follows:

- Firstly we carry out a valuation of all the assets separately, including the goodwill. Adding the values together will give us the sum of the parts.
- We then look at the level of profits to see what return they will give on our capital investment. If we pay that amount for the business, is the return on invested capital reasonable?

Goodwill

We have already looked at valuing goodwill in the previous section. In the case of businesses with tangible assets goodwill is valued in exactly the same way.

There is, however, one difference in cases where the assets include ownership of the property from which the business is run. In such cases there will be no rent charged in the accounts and, so that we do not double count value, we need to deduct from the adjusted profit figure the amount of notional rent used when we valued the property.

The easiest way to explain why is to think of the property purchase and business purchase as separate transactions. If Party A bought the business, and Party B bought the property, Party B would charge Party A the rent. In that situation Party A would buy the business at a goodwill value that was calculated on annual profits reduced by the rent. The combined prices paid by Party A and Party B would, therefore, be the property value plus the goodwill valued on a profit from which the rent was deducted. That is, therefore, the total price you should pay.

Valuation of the business as a whole

We can only look at this by way of examples which you can adapt to your situation.

Let's take an example of a freehold healthfood store.

- As is normal, the fixtures and fittings are not valued separately from the goodwill, which on the basis of profits of £40,000 per annum has been valued at £70,000 (1.75 YP).
- On the basis of a notional rent of £15,000 the property has been valued at £125,000.

If we deduct the notional rent of £15,000 from profits we are left with an adjusted profit of £25,000. Using a YP of 1.75 this revises the goodwill valuation to £43,750, which when added to the property produces an overall value of the business on a freehold basis of £168,750.

Is it a good buy at that price? Well, because we have valued it in a logical way, it probably is. The final check you should make is the overall return on the capital employed. When you calculate the overall return on invested capital, the result should be at least 15–20 per cent.

In this case, the £40,000 annual income (£25,000 profit made by the business and £15,000 notional rental income for the property) is a return of a shade under 24 per cent per annum on an investment of £168,750.

Let's take another example – a freehold engineering works.

- Annual profit is £30,000 and goodwill valued at £45,000 (1.5 YP).
- The business operates from a modern adaptable warehouse type property valued at £110,000 based on a notional rent of £15,000 p.a.
- Special machinery is valued at £45,000.

If we deduct the notional rent from profit the goodwill value becomes £22,500 (£15,000 profit at a 1.5 YP). Adding this to the property and machinery we get an overall price of £177,500. At this price the net income (business profit and notional rent) of £30,000 represents a return of a little less than 17 per cent. This is just within the target range of 15 to 20 per cent, but on the low side, especially for a higher risk business such as engineering, where a 20 per cent minimum expectation would not be unreasonable.

Possibly the seller would agree to sell for £150,000 which would mean achieving a 20 per cent return. But let's look at another possibility.

If you bought the business on a leasehold basis you would pay £45,000 for the machinery and £22,500 for goodwill, a total of £67,500. The profit, after rent of £15,000 would be £15,000, a return of 22 per cent. The financial risk is lower, having outlaid much less and, although the property is desirable, you're not missing much because the potential for capital gain on a property of this nature is nowhere near as high as it is in the housing market. There is now a return of 22 per cent which is much more acceptable.

It is possible that the vendor might be willing to keep the property and rent it to you, or it might be possible for him to sell it separately to a property investment company. The other possibility worth looking at would be for you to do a sale and leaseback deal with a finance company.

Unless you are particularly keen to own a property, for example if you have spare funds that need a better home than a savings account, these options are always worth considering, because industrial or warehouse type properties rarely have a particularly high potential for capital gain in the way residential ones normally do.

Hotels and guesthouses

In the case of medium-sized hotels, say 12 rooms and upwards, the only way to look at value is to capitalise the profits at about 15 per cent (6.5 YP). Whatever the bricks and mortar value under a different use may be, it is the hotel business that has to earn your living from the building. Less than a 15 per cent return will be insufficient to pay your mortgage as well as give you a reasonable income for your efforts.

With smaller guesthouses, where the owner's main accommodation is included, and often it is a business only run during the season, possibly the best way to approach it is to put a property value on the residential part, and then add the value of goodwill at 6.5 YP.

Care homes

Care homes are too specialised to go into here in too much detail.

The problem with care homes is the minefield of legislation and constantly changing regulations on staffing and premises. If you have no previous experience you will need specialist help and, unless you have suitable qualifications, the authorities will require you to employ a manager.

You will find the authorities very helpful, since they are always keen to ensure that new owners take over without any illusions as to what is expected. You will need to find out from them whether the home has been well run to date and, if not, in what ways it has been below par. You will especially need to check with them whether there are any alterations that will be needed to be made to the premises to maintain the registration, and whether it is likely that additional staffing will be required in the future. The authorities are often lenient with existing owners about property improvements they would like, especially where substantial sums of money will be needed to be spent. However, when a new owner comes along they see it as a golden opportunity to insist on these improvements being made straightaway.

You will need the authority's approval to be registered as the new owner of the home, so a formal interview will in any event be required before you complete the purchase. However, before getting into too much expense on professional fees, it is wise to arrange for an informal meeting to ascertain any likely problems or unexpected expenditure at an early stage.

Once you have ascertained the situation from the authorities, you will need to consider any necessary adjustments to the profit figures to cover additional staff costs, if any.

You will also need very carefully to consider what they say about the premises. It could be that it is not physically possible to change the building to meet their requirements without reducing the number of beds, in which case the profit will have to be reworked at a lower turnover. In addition, the cost of necessary building works will have to be estimated and deducted from the final offer.

Care homes rarely have an alternative use and, when they do, they require a lot of money spent to adapt them, so a bricks and mortar value is not a good way to proceed. The only sensible way to approach it is to calculate an adjusted profit, and capitalise it at 15 per cent (6.5 YP) as for hotels.

Chapter 7:

Verifying the Information You Have Been Given

Although you will have been supplied with copies of accounts, it is vital to check that the trading information you have been given is fully truthful.

At the early stages of your discussions with the vendor you clearly have to take the figures at face value, but before you are committed you must check them out as best you can. The professionals call this process 'due diligence'.

You cannot simply rely on the accountants who produced the accounts. Firstly, you do not know what level of verification they carried out in producing them. A full audit is rarely required these days, unless it is a limited company with a high turnover. The accountants will always include a certificate in the accounts which will state the level of checking they have done. Often the certificate states that 'in producing the accounts we have relied on information supplied by the proprietors', and goes on to state that no independent verification has been carried out. In other words, rely on these accounts at your own risk. Most accountants do check things somewhat, but unless there is a full audit certificate you could never successfully sue them if you relied on accounts that you subsequently discovered were untrue.

In any event, the latest annual accounts will cover a period that ended a long time ago, so you will need to verify the management trading figures you have been given for the period since the last annual accounts – these are the latest and definitely most important since they cover current trading.

So, what should you do? Obviously you cannot check every bookkeeping entry, but there is much you can do to satisfy yourself.

You can ask your accountants to do this for you and, if the

sums involved are substantial relative to your financial situation, then having them involved would be a wise precaution that is highly recommended. However, it is also highly recommended that you maintain an involvement in the process yourself, especially if your accountants are not experienced in running businesses themselves. Many accountants, whilst excellent technically in accountancy, are not sufficiently streetwise not to be taken in by a dishonest businessperson setting out to pull the wool over their eyes. Therefore, get involved yourself, and ensure that at least the steps outlined in this chapter are taken to verify the trading figures.

Ask to speak with the existing accountants to the business

If the vendor has nothing to hide he should have no problem with this. If you are doing the verification without your accountants, the current accountants are probably hoping that they will continue to be doing your accounts when you take over, so they are likely to be helpful. Engage them in chat as much as possible to see what general comments transpire.

They will probably know quite a bit about the business, and you will gain an overall impression about their professionalism. Ask them what they do to produce the accounts. They might tell you that they effectively write up the accounts from scratch, in which case if you trust them as people you probably trust the accounts. On the other hand, they may say that they get books written up by the owner which they convert into final accounts for the taxman, but they do little more. If it is the latter, ask them how good the accounting systems are at the business. If they say, 'You don't have to worry about John, he accounts for everything down to the last penny,' then fine, but if they are cagey you have been warned!

Depending on how much the accountants do, it will be appropriate to undertake all or some of the following tasks with the accountants or with the owner:

Check the bank accounts

Ask to see the original bank account statements for at least the last two years. You can check a lot of things looking at these:

- Turnover – add up the credits going through the account. Do they roughly amount to the sales figures you have been given?
- Expenses – look at the direct debits/standing orders. Rent, electricity/gas bills, telephone bills, business rates, etc., will be paid through the account. Do they look similar to the amounts shown in the accounts?
- Bounced cheques! Does the account look healthy? If the owner is selling because he can't make ends meet, it will show. It doesn't mean that you don't want to buy the business, but you need to know why he is under pressure. It may be entirely personal financial pressures, in which case you may have a really good opportunity here.
- Question any large unusual amounts.

Check the VAT returns

The owner should have kept copies, which will show turnover declared and expenses claimed for VAT. If you are not familiar with VAT returns, reading Chapter 14, VAT – an Overview, will give you an understanding of what you are looking at.

You will need to review the returns for all the periods covered by the accounts (at least two years if it is an established business). The total sales declared on the returns should be consistent with the accounts you have been given.

The returns will show the net amount paid in VAT to the Government, or refunds received. Double check that the returns are genuine by checking that there are paid cheques, or credit entries, in the bank statements for each of those amounts.

Check purchase invoices

Check that volumes are as expected, and that prices are as well. If the vendor has told you that toys make a 33 per cent mark-up for example, look at some invoices and check the unit prices against sale prices on the shelves.

If you have been told that the business receives credit from its suppliers, check whether the invoices indicate the credit terms you have been told the business gets. Most companies show the due date, as well as the invoice date, on their invoices. You can do a quick calculation to check the overall average credit received from suppliers, the formula being:

$$\text{average days' credit received} \quad = \quad \frac{\text{total creditors x 365}}{\text{annual purchases}}$$

So if annual purchases are £250,000 and total creditors outstanding stand at £65,000:

$$\frac{65,000 \times 365}{250,000} \quad = \quad 95 \text{ days}$$

Obviously this is only a rough guide as there could be variations according to the time in the month the calculation is done, and it is no substitution for a detailed physical check of the original invoices. However, it will certainly show up any significant variation from what you have been told.

In this example, if the vendor told the purchaser he is getting three months he is telling the truth. However, if your research shows that your vendor is getting shorter credit than he told you, recheck your cash flow forecast because you will probably need more working capital than you thought.

Check, by adding up invoices if necessary, whether the business is highly dependent on one or two suppliers. If a large percentage of purchases come from one or two suppliers then this dependency may not be too healthy. If other suppliers are around, and could be used instead, then clearly there is no worry. However, if finding alternative suppliers could be difficult, you will need to consider the potential risks. Suppose one of the major suppliers goes out of business or stops selling what you are buying? What if he jacks up the price when he sees there is a new owner?

For most businesses, finding new suppliers will not be a problem. However, if you discover that the business you are looking at does have an unhealthy dependency on certain suppliers, you may feel that this vulnerability makes the business too risky to contemplate buying.

Spend some time at the business

The vendor may be worried about staff finding out that he is selling, and may not be keen for you to spend time there for that reason. However, if you can, be around and watch what is going on. Keep a mental note of what is going through the till, for example. If it's a pub or café, it should be easy to sit in a corner and just watch and listen – are the staff good, the customers happy, is the till ringing up as much as you would expect?

For businesses with trade customers

You need to know how dependent the business is on selling to a few large customers. This is a much more common problem than dependency on suppliers.

Ask the vendor who the biggest customers are and what percentage of total sales they represent. Ask to see the records to verify the answers.

Obviously, a business that has a high proportion of its trade with a few large customers is much more risky than one with a wide spread of small customers. If one or two customers account for 25 per cent or more of sales, was this what you were expecting? Are those customers loyal to the vendor personally and likely to go elsewhere when he leaves?

If the business sells on credit, you need to know whether the term of credit given is what you have been told. It is easy for the vendor to say that his terms are thirty days but, if most of the customers are taking sixty days to pay, he is in reality giving sixty days. A quick check on the overall situation can be easily calculated. The formula for working out the average number of days' credit given is:

$$\text{average days' credit received} = \frac{\text{total debtors} \times 365}{\text{annual sales}}$$

If the total outstanding debtors are £50,000 and the annual turnover is £450,000 the calculation is:

$$\frac{50,000 \times 365}{450,000} = 40 \text{ days}$$

Obviously forty days is an average. If particular customers are being very slow to pay, perhaps you should look into whether they are worth having. If they amount to a significant proportion of turnover, you may wish to recalculate what you think the business is worth.

You should be able to verify whether the business has many

customers who are very slow payers. The vendor should be able to supply you with a report of outstanding invoices showing how old they are. If their invoices are factored, and the credit control function is handled by the factoring company, there should be reports produced by the factoring company to look at.

Remember, if you have done your cash flow calculations based on the business giving thirty days' credit, and in reality they are giving an average of forty-five days, you are going to need extra working capital.

Chapter 8:

Negotiating the Deal

The price

Hopefully the earlier chapters on assessing the business and valuing it will have given you the ability to marshal the ammunition for negotiating the price. There is not much to be added here, except to reinforce the point made in an earlier chapter about not overpaying just because you are keen. Businesses are not like houses, in the sense that, generally, they do not grow in value over time just by being there. If you overpaid for your house by 10 per cent five years ago, it is unlikely to be significant today. Businesses, however, do not appreciate by very much unless they are expanded or made much more profitable. Therefore, in the longer term, people usually regret overpaying.

Ongoing support

Never be afraid to ask the vendor to be available to provide advice and help for a period after takeover, especially if it is your first business.

Obviously, what he will be able to do will depend on what he is doing next. If he is retiring nearby there is no reason why he could not be available by phone, and possibly to come in from time to time. If he is moving to Spain in three months, obviously he will only be available until then. If he is taking over another business in another part of the country, then clearly he will be able to do less for you.

However, you can usually expect him to be available to some extent, and you should be very sceptical about the motives of a vendor who flatly refuses.

Stock

Please see Chapter 13, Paying for Stock and Debtors, which covers a number of issues that you should consider at this point in the negotiations.

Debtors

Similarly, if debtors are a part of the business, read Chapter 13.

Chapter 9:

Types of Finance

In essence there are three main sources of money to fund a business venture:

- Equity (or capital).
- Debt.
- Grants.

Equity

Equity is the term used by financiers to describe the capital invested in the business by the business owners from their own resources.

The advantage to the business of equity is that there is no interest charge, and a return is only paid to the investors if the business is generating money (*no duck – no dinner!*).

For the single person or couple buying a small business on their own, there are really only two sources of equity:

- Funds from personal wealth.
- Profits generated by the business after takeover (which are obviously not available to fund the initial purchase of the business, but can contribute to financing expansion further down the road).

As we shall see when we discuss debt, because equity is free to the business, providers of debt finance like to see a reasonable amount of financial commitment from the business owners. If you are short of funds, it may be necessary to seek additional investors to provide equity to top up yours, possibly by bringing in a business partner. We discuss later how to seek out the other various providers of equity that exist, but it has to be said here that professional investors are not interested in investing in the bog standard small business.

We discussed the aspects of assessing how much equity you can afford to invest in Chapter 4, How Much Should You Spend on a Business? That chapter describes preliminary calculations to get you going on finding a suitable business. If you have not read that chapter, or do not recall its contents in detail, please read it before proceeding further with this one. How to discover how much equity will actually be needed in a specific case is discussed in the following paragraphs and the next chapter.

Debt

There are various types of debt, some general in nature, and some tailored to a particular purpose. It is important for the ongoing health of the business to ensure that it is funded appropriately.

As already stated, providers of debt finance like to see a reasonable financial investment contributed by the owners of the business. This is because:

- They do not like to take all the risk – if the owner has no money at stake he could walk with impunity at the first sign of trouble.
- Equity money is free – as already stated, equity investors get nothing unless the business generates money.
- In the case of insolvency the debt is paid back before equity.

Lenders describe the relationship between debt and equity as the 'debt to equity ratio' or 'gearing'.

If you buy a business for £100,000, borrowing £75,000 and paying £25,000 from your own savings, the debt to equity ratio (or gearing) is 3:1.

Different lenders look to different maximums for the debt to equity ratio, often setting separate criteria for each type of transaction. In calculating the ratio they include all sources of debt, not just their own.

The other main consideration for lenders is the available profit to service the debt, often referred to as 'interest coverage' or 'debt service ratio'. If they consider that the forecast profit is too low in relation to the anticipated level of interest and repayments, they will not lend.

There are many different types of debt, and only some will

probably be relevant to your case. In the next chapter we will be looking at the following types of debt finance:

General

Term loans.
Overdrafts.
Business cards.
Government Loan Guarantee Scheme.
Trade creditors.

Asset linked

Invoice finance (for businesses that sell on credit).
Vehicle finance.
Commercial mortgages (for business property).
Plant and equipment finance.
Leasing (for vehicles or equipment)

Some of the types of finance are rather complicated and it is pointless reading through them all unless they could be relevant to your type of business. That is, unless this book is the best bedtime reading you have, of course!

Grants

Grants are generally only made available for encouraging invest-ment in new business projects in areas of the country where unemployment is a major problem, or in particular industries that it is in the public interest to encourage – solar energy, for example. If you are buying an existing business it is highly unlikely that you will be eligible for grants, and it is beyond the remit of this book to provide information on the myriad schemes that are available. However, if you think what you are doing could be eligible for such assistance you should contact your local *Business Link* who will guide you in the right direction (see page 15 for more information on *Business Link*).

Chapter 10:

How to Raise Debt and Equity Finance

RAISING DEBT FINANCE

There are many ways of arranging business finance apart from going along to your local high street bank. For anybody who is not particularly financially aware, some good advice is going to be needed. However, bear these two very important overriding considerations in mind from the start:

- Financial institutions lend money because they are confident in the ability of the people running the business.
- Financial institutions these days are fiercely competitive for *good* business.

Notice the emphasis on *good*. The important point to make is this. Banks and other financiers are very keen to attract good business, and will be very competitive in their efforts to do so. But, if the business is less than top-rate, they will either turn it down or charge much higher rates. You have to bear in mind that one bad loan wipes out the profit from ten good ones. So what does this mean to you?

It means that you need to convince the financiers you approach that, whilst you may be new to running a business, you are clearly someone who has thought it all through very carefully. You are someone who knows what he is doing, understands the fundamentals of the business being acquired, and is, therefore, probably going to be a success in the longer term.

This cannot be done by handing over the whole thing to an advisor to arrange. Yes he has good contacts, yes using them is a good idea, but you are not going to get the best deal unless you involve *yourself* in the presentation of the case. You need to check all the information that he is presenting, and be available to answer any questions that may be raised by potential lenders.

Using advisors

For the purpose of this subject we will look at two groups of advisor: brokers and financial/business advisors.

Brokers

Brokers make their living by maintaining good contacts with the hundreds of institutions that provide all the different types of business finance available in the UK.

They keep registers of the types of finance and the standard terms that the different institutions are prepared to offer, such as:

- Which types of finance they provide.
- Minimum and maximum amounts they offer.
- Which types of businesses they lend to.
- Their lending criteria such as maximum debt to equity ratio, minimum security requirements, valuation requirements, etc.
- Interest rates and length of loan term.

There is no doubt that being able to tap into this data can save you a lot of legwork – indeed you couldn't really do it thoroughly yourself. However, brokers generally do have their limitations:

- *Many charge substantial non-refundable up-front fees.* Although some institutions pay an introduction fee to brokers, a large number do not. In any event, since so many deals fail to go through, the brokers need to get paid for their time whether they are successful or not.
- *Many of them have good contacts, but little presentation skills.* You generally cannot depend on a broker to prepare a professional presentation for you. They often need the proposition to be prepared for them so they can identify the institutions that are most likely to help and submit it to them. They are rarely able to prepare cash flows and business plans for you.
- *Some institutions do not like dealing with brokers.* Most notable in this respect are the high street banks. Although they acknowledge that brokers are a good source of new business,

the banks purely regard them as introducers, and do not pay commissions. Whilst they will deal in general terms with the broker at the very beginning, they do so only to establish that, on first look, it appears to be a case worthy of consideration. Once they have established their interest, they will want to see you at an early stage. They know that the brokers do not vet you in any way and they will want your answers to their questions, not the brokers'.

Finding brokers is easy. Many advertise in *Daltons Weekly* and the business-to-business sections of national and regional newspapers. *Yellow Pages* and *Thomson* are good sources, of course, and you can use the search engines on the Internet. If you can get a recommendation, from a friend or from your accountant, then so much the better. If you are buying the business through a business transfer agent, his agency will probably have a finance department or, if not, will have a working relationship with an independent broker.

Unless brokers have been recommended to you, checking them out is not so easy. The first key question, of course, is what they are going to charge you. For the reasons already stated, you will find that most will want to charge an initial fee, whatever the outcome, and probably then a pro-rata fee based on the amount successfully raised once an offer of financing is received. But how do you decide if and when to punt an up-front fee? Mainly you will have to go on instinct as to who seems the most professional, but why not ask them to provide the names of a couple of recent clients that you can speak with?

Financial/Business advisors

Under this heading I include independent advisors who are able to offer business advice, such as developing a business plan, advising on the best way to finance the business, and assisting you to prepare the presentation for the lenders.

Often these advisors are part of a firm of accountants, or they may be individuals such as former bankers who have the necessary experience. If you need an introduction, you could do no better than to speak to your local *Business Link*.

If, when you have read through the following sections on financing a couple of times, you find it a bit mind-boggling, you

should definitely seek the assistance of an advisor before
approaching any institutions, because first impressions are all
important.

Business transfer agents

All of the leading business transfer agents offer a financing service
and will have a department familiar with leading lenders in the
same way as the brokers referred to above. If you are buying your
business through a business transfer agent, this is probably the
best place to start. The institutions tend to have more respect for
such departments because obviously they are specialists and,
through the parent organisation, have a good knowledge of the
business being purchased.

Going direct

If you have the confidence, and there is every reason you should
have if you follow the steps in this chapter, approach the local
banks directly, and any other institutions for that matter.

However, before doing so, prepare yourself by going through
the different types of financing available. Ask for a preliminary
meeting with the business banker. At that meeting tell him that
you are proposing to make an application for finance, and ask
him for all the necessary forms to be completed. He will no doubt
ask some general questions and give you some good pointers as to
what information he will be expecting to receive, as well as an
indication in general terms of what he is likely to be able to offer
you if your proposal is favourable.

However, make it obvious that you regard this as a preliminary
meeting and that you will be asking for a further meeting after
you have prepared a full presentation.

Preparing the presentation

Even if you are using a business advisor, work on the presentation
with him by feeding him with as much of the information
described below as you can.

These are the general headings that your presentation should
cover. The level of emphasis on each will vary in individual cases:

●   Details of the new owners.

- Description of the business.
- The management and staffing.
- The financing plan.
- Cash flow projections.
- Historical accounts.

Details of the new owners

This should include a brief history of your career to date and details of your financial circumstances.

Do not worry if you have never run a business before. The lenders accept that we all have to start somewhere, and are mostly looking at how professionally you are approaching this venture.

Do not exaggerate. If your house may just fetch £175,000 on a lucky day, but is more realistically worth £160,000, put it in at £160,000. If it's important, the manager will check it, and there is nothing that looks worse to a banker than finding statements in a presentation that mislead. It will make him sceptical about the accuracy of the other information you have included.

Description of the business

A general overview of the key elements of the business including, as applicable:

- General description of the location.
- Type of clientele/customers.
- Turnover and profits to date.
- Price paid.
- The competition, if any.
- Future plans.
- Why you consider this to be a particularly good purchase.

The management and staffing

- General information on staff being taken over, such as experience, length of service, etc.
- Who will manage the business day-to-day?
- What will the owner's involvement be?
- What controls are in place over cash and stock?

The financing plan

- Total investment required.
- The amount of equity being invested.
- Debt finance sought – what types and how much of each.

Cash flow forecast

If you are buying a business with a cash trade evenly spread over the year, the cash flow forecast is less important and relatively easy to prepare. Indeed, provided you have ample finance to make the initial purchase of the business and stock, you will probably never need more finance unless you propose to diversify at some stage, or some totally unforeseeable circumstance arises. In such cases a cash flow forecast at this stage has little value and may not be requested.

However, in other cases, cash flow can vary considerably on a week-to-week or month-to-month basis, and it is important to identify the maximum likely funding requirement to ensure that it is covered. This is the purpose of the cash flow forecast. Undoubtedly it is the hardest bit of the presentation to prepare, particularly if you are acquiring a business that is seasonal. If you have no accounting experience, you will probably need professional help with this. If you have a little accounting knowledge, the leading banks do have free computer programs to take you through it step by step.

The cash flow forecast is essentially a chronological table of cash movements in and out of the business on a weekly or monthly basis. It is not the same as sales and purchases in the same period. If you purchase stock on the first of January and sell it on the second, your cash position will depend on the terms. If you pay cash for the stock, and sell it for cash you are out of pocket for one day. If you buy the stock on thirty days' credit and sell it for cash the next day, you will be cash neutral for a day and then in pocket for twenty-nine days until you pay the supplier. That will give you the money to fund other transactions. If you buy the stock on thirty days' credit, and sell it on sixty days' credit you will be cash neutral for thirty days, no cash having changed hands, and then out of pocket for the next thirty days, after you pay the supplier, until the customer pays you. In each case you should eventually finish up cash positive by the profit margin, but, as you can see, in the meantime the amount of cash you need to have available varies. When you prepare the cash flow forecast, the appropriate payment terms are included, as are different sales and purchase volumes at different times of the year, and thus it will take all the variations into account.

The cash flow projection should also include the cost of buying the business at the outset and the cost of any additional capital items that will need to be purchased during the year. It should also include anticipated general expenses such as rent and utilities as and when they fall due. As a result, it shows a prediction of how much maximum overall funding is likely to be needed at any given time over the period it covers.

The presentation should not only contain the cash flow figures themselves, but also the assumptions you have used in preparing them, such as rate of sales growth, price increases in sales and expenses, suppliers' payment terms, payment terms offered to customers, etc.

Whilst all the leading banks have forms for manually preparing cash flow forecasts, the forecast is best prepared on a computer spreadsheet program such as Microsoft Excel, Microsoft Works or Lotus 123, and this is how all professional advisors would do it. Once set up, these programs automatically do all the mathematical calculations for you, making it easy to change assumptions and see what the effects are. For example, you could increase sales prices by 10 per cent and, without having to redo all the calculations manually, see the knock-on effects on profitability and cash flow and hence financing requirements. You can give a copy on disk to the bank and they can do their own 'what if' experiments like this.

Historical accounts

You will need to attach the historical accounting information received from the vendors. You should include the accounts for the last three years, along with the management figures covering the period since the date of the latest annual accounts.

The lender will look at these figures in detail to assess the ability of the business to cover the cost of the finance being sought. It is a good idea to write a summary of your findings and adjustments when you reviewed the accounts for the purpose of your valuation (as per the sections on reviewing the accounts in

Chapter 6). It is also a good idea to state what steps you have taken to verify the accounts (as per Chapter 7, Verifying the Information You Have Been Given). Not only will it answer a lot of his questions without the need to ask them, it also shows him how professional you have been in reaching your decision to buy this particular business.

Deciding what types of finance to raise and how much

If you look through the descriptions of different types of debt finance that follow on page 120 you will become familiar with the types of finance available to your business.

It should also be clear to you that it is important for the financial stability of your business to ensure that you raise the right mix of finance.

The cash flow forecast described above will enable you to determine the hardcore funding requirement and the fluctuating working capital requirement (see page 124). This will enable you to decide how much in longer-term finance and how much on overdraft, respectively, need to be raised.

With regard to the longer-term requirement, particularly if you are raising a relatively large amount of money, it may pay to raise as much as you can from the specialised sources, such as leasing or vehicle finance, to minimise your demands on the general lenders.

If you are buying a business with a freehold or long leasehold property, explore the commercial mortgage market first. Your local bank will offer such a facility for sure, but check other sources as well.

If you are a homeowner you should also consider this. Wherever and however you raise the money you will be personally liable and, if it all goes pear-shaped, your personal assets, including your house, could be used to repay the debts. Even if you take an unsecured personal loan, if you default, the lender may be able to obtain legal security over your house through the court. Therefore, if you have plenty of equity in the house, consider raising extra on the mortgage. The interest will be tax deductible, and it will be the cheapest money you can find.

The first rule to observe is this – and for your ongoing banking relationships it is very important – BE SURE TO RAISE ENOUGH FINANCE.

People often make the mistake of thinking that the less they ask for, the better the chances of getting a 'yes'. In reality, nothing makes a financier more nervous than when shortly after agreeing an initial finance package he receives a request for an increase because more funding is needed.

- Firstly, it makes him look bad to his superiors because he did not pick up the fact that you got it wrong.
- Secondly, he wonders, if you got it wrong before, have you still got it wrong now?
- Thirdly, he wonders, what else did you get wrong?

Financiers regard themselves as conservative people, and have respect for clients who are careful in their business dealings. Build in a contingency of at least 10 per cent for unforeseen circumstances. Better still, before you finalise how much overall funding to raise, play around with the assumptions in the cash flow forecast to see the effect on the funding requirement if, for example, sales volumes or prices are 5 per cent lower than expected. Increase the total funding sought to cover that or any other similar eventualities you think of.

If the financier sees that you have built in a safety margin in this way, he will not think you are greedy, he will be pleased to see that you are being cautious, and that you will not be financially de-stabilised by the slightest knock.

Security

Special finance such as commercial mortgages or vehicle loans are naturally secured on the asset they are linked to. In the case of leasing, the legal ownership of the asset is vested in the institution, not you.

For the more general types of finance, term loans and overdrafts, the institutions will normally seek security as well.

If a property is being acquired, they will want a legal charge over it, unless of course you have funded that part of the acquisition elsewhere. They may well also look to the goodwill value of the business, as confirmed by an independent valuation commissioned by the lender but paid for by you.

They may also seek security over assets such as the debtors and stock. The choice of legal entity you elect to trade under may be relevant here, especially as regards stock, because it is not really possible for an institution to take effective security over stock except where the borrower is a limited company. If the stock is likely to be an important part of the security on offer, see Chapter 11, Choosing a Legal Entity for Your Business.

Personal guarantees

If you are trading as a sole trader, all the debt will be in your name and you are therefore fully liable as a matter of course. If you are in partnership with one or more others, the lenders will require each partner to be fully liable for the entire debt. This is normally the position under the law of the land anyway.

If you are trading as a limited company, they will probably want personal guarantees from the owners. When you considered the legal entity and chose to use a limited company, it may have been because you wanted to restrict your personal financial liability. Lending institutions are aware that as a matter of course you are not liable personally for the debts of the company. At the same time, it is you that they are supporting and they do not see any intrinsic merit in the company itself. They will therefore insist that you personally guarantee the facilities granted to the company. If the company is owned by yourself and your spouse/partner, you will both individually be required fully to guarantee the whole of the debt. If you have one or more co-owners of the company who are not members of your immediate family, the lender would again normally expect all shareholders individually to guarantee the full debt. In other words, if you are going into the business fifty/fifty with a friend and it goes wrong, you couldn't pay half and leave the bank to suffer the loss if the friend was unable to pay the other half. In legal parlance this is called *joint and several liability*.

TYPES OF DEBT FINANCE

Term loans

Term loans are a flexible means to finance the *hardcore* financial requirement of the business not covered by equity.

The total funding requirement of most businesses goes up and down on a daily basis as working capital requirements fluctuate. For example, a greetings card company will have its highest need for funding just before Christmas when it has had to stock all its outlets with Christmas cards. After Christmas when they have been sold and the cash has been banked, the company's funding requirement will be at the low point for the year. When bankers refer to the *hardcore* financial requirement of the business they mean the minimum amount of funding that will permanently be required, even at the point of lowest need.

Term loans can also be used for financing the purchase of equipment. However, for larger purchases of equipment a finance lease may be a better (and/or more tax efficient) alternative.

We are all familiar with the general concept of term loans, but there are a few points to consider when negotiating with lenders.

Amount

The amount lenders will advance usually depends on the security provided and the interest cover provided by the business profits. The advantage of a term loan over, say, an overdraft is that it is long-term in nature. In general, it is therefore to your benefit to place as much as possible of the total funding being arranged on a term loan basis, because that way you minimise the pressures on cash flow.

Repayment holiday

In the early days you will want to minimise financial pressures as much as possible. Often banks will agree to an initial period of up to two or three years when they will only debit interest and will not require any repayment of the loan. Do not be afraid to ask for this, because they can see the sense of it, and like dealing with cautious customers.

Loan length

Negotiate as long a loan term as you can, although all lenders will have a maximum term laid down under lending policy.

Interest rate

You probably have little bargaining power at the beginning, but as you prove yourself you should be able to negotiate them down after a year or two. If they say that they are putting you on a higher rate because you are new to running a business, make it clear that you will expect a reduction in the future when all has gone well.

VARIABLE RATE

Interest rates on business term loans typically range from 3 per cent to 6 per cent over base rate.

FIXED RATE

It is often possible to negotiate a fixed rate, although there is usually a minimum size of loan for this. Rates can be fixed for periods of one to ten years.

Fixed rates offer the advantage of certainty of how much you will have to pay each month, but remember there is likely to be a penalty if you repay early – upon resale of the business for example – so it may not be sensible to fix the rate for too long. It is always possible to negotiate a further fixed rate period when the first one ends, though it will relate to the rate then currently prevailing.

Arrangement fee

There is usually an arrangement fee payable at the beginning of the loan. This is normally between 1 per cent and 2 per cent (high street banks typically 1.25 per cent to 1.5 per cent).

There may also be fees for taking security.

Security

PERSONAL GUARANTEES

Almost invariably required where the borrowing is not in your personal name.

OTHER SECURITY

Usually required, unless the bank is happy to lend against your personal standing.

Where security is required, banks and finance houses will lend up to a percentage of the value of the security offered. Individual institutions set different limits, but the following are typical percentages:

Freehold property	70–85 per cent, in exceptional cases higher.
Goodwill	70 per cent.
Debtors	70–75 per cent.
Stock	50–60 per cent.

If you are able to offer additional security they may go higher, provided interest cover (see below) is adequate.

See Chapter 11, Choosing a Legal Entity for Your Business, if stock is to form part of the security.

Interest cover

Some finance houses only look to security. Banks, however, will also be keen to see that interest and repayments are comfortable given the profit level of the business after the owner's private drawings have been taken. In assessing this, banks look at how many times the net profit after drawings covers the loan servicing. Policies differ, but 1.5 times cover is usually a minimum requirement.

Insurance

You can obtain insurance to cover interest and capital repayments in the event of accident or sickness. See Chapter 18. Often lenders insist on this.

Sources of term loans

In addition to the high street banks, there are many other term loan lenders, some owned by foreign banks.

Overdrafts

We are all familiar with the concept of being allowed to overdraw the current account, and agreed overdraft limits are a common means of financing businesses.

However, although they are normally reviewed on an annual

basis, it must be remembered that overdraft limits can be withdrawn with immediate effect, so it is important to understand how the banks view them.

If you have read the section on term loans you will have seen how the term loan is intended to finance the 'hardcore' financing requirement of the business. The overdraft is intended to finance the working capital needs of the business and/or funding needs of a temporary nature.

An example of a need of a temporary nature, where an overdraft would be the obvious solution, would be when it is necessary to pay VAT on a major purchase and a refund will be received at the end of the VAT quarter.

The working capital of a business is the capital investment needed to fund the day-to-day working assets of the business:

- Cash.
- Stock.
- Work-in-progress.
- Debtors.

These are called the current assets. Sometimes they are also referred to as the circulating assets: *cash is used to buy stock; stock is sold; cash is received in payment; cash is used to buy new stock; and so on.*

Businesses often buy stock on credit from suppliers who become creditors.

The net of the current assets minus creditors is known as net working capital.

This working capital requirement will fluctuate from day to day, going up as stock is bought and the creditors are paid, and going down as the debtors pay outstanding invoices or cash sales go into the till. In the bank's eyes the current account in a healthy well-funded business should fluctuate regularly during the month from a low of being overdrawn fairly close to the agreed limit, to a high point when it is actually in credit.

If the current account is permanently overdrawn by at least £5,000, then £5,000 of the hardcore financing requirement of the business is being funded on overdraft and ought to be refinanced on a term loan basis.

If the *hardcore* overdraft is going up and up, the bank may well become alarmed because either the business is making losses or too much is being withdrawn by the owner for personal drawings.

It is important, therefore, to ensure that only the truly fluctuating part of the overall funding requirement is met by way of overdraft, and that the hardcore requirement is covered by one or more of the longer-term sources of finance. When you are formulating your initial proposal to the bank, an examination of the cash flow forecast will show you what level of overdraft facility would be appropriate.

If the business you are acquiring enjoys trade credit from its suppliers, an important factor to consider is whether in the early days you may not be given as much trade credit as the vendor has been accustomed to. Before deciding on how much to raise by overdraft, read the section about trade creditors on page 136.

Terms and conditions for overdrafts are similar in many respects to those for term loans, and will include the following:

Interest rate

Like other forms of finance, overdraft interest rates vary according to the perceived risk, security available, and track record to date. They typically range from 2 per cent to 6 per cent over base rate. Once you have a track record you can look to negotiate the rate down.

Repayment

In theory, an overdraft facility is repayable immediately upon demand, but a bank would only normally make a formal demand if there were problems with the account. In normal circumstances, the overdraft facility would be reviewed on an annual basis and, all being well, would continue for a further year.

Security

Sometimes the bank will require security, as with other forms of finance.

PERSONAL GUARANTEES

Almost invariably required where the borrowing is not in your personal name.

OTHER SECURITY

Usually required, unless the bank is happy to lend against your personal standing.

Where security is required, banks and finance houses will lend up to a percentage of the value of the security offered. Individual institutions set different limits, but the following are typical percentages:

Freehold property 70–85 per cent, in exceptional cases higher.
Goodwill   70 per cent.
Debtors   70–75 per cent.
Stock   50–60 per cent.

If you are able to offer additional security, they may go higher, provided interest cover (see below) is adequate. See Chapter 11, Choosing a Legal Entity for Your Business, if stock is to form part of the security.

Insurance

You can obtain insurance to cover interest and capital repayments in the event of accident or sickness. See Chapter 18. Usually lenders insist on this.

Sources

Overdrafts are available from a number of smaller and foreign owned banks but, unless you are located in a major city, the only practical source will be the major high street banks. Although you can normally pay into an account held elsewhere via a high street bank, they charge for this (in addition to the charges you will be paying to your own bank), so you would need to check that the overall bank charges do not wipe out any gain in lower interest rates if you use a lender other than a high street bank.

Business cards

Business cards work in a similar way to personal credit cards except that the full balance has to be paid off at the end of each month.

Unlike personal cards, it is possible to issue cards to various employees, each with a limit set by you (obviously the aggregate total of the individual limits you set cannot exceed the overall limit set for you by the bank).

However, the most useful feature of the business card to the small-business person is the ability to use it to pay for purchases of stock and other supplies, particularly in the early days when it may be difficult to obtain credit terms from suppliers.

As the balance is paid off each month, there is no interest charge, unless the card is used for cash withdrawals when the charge is similar to personal credit cards.

There is, however, an annual fee, dependent on the number of cards issued (£100 per annum is not untypical for two cards).

So that they can check their transactions, each cardholder gets a monthly statement showing just his own transactions. The business owner gets a copy of all the statements, together with an overall summary.

SECURITY

The banks do not generally take security solely for business card facilities, but the agreed limit will be taken into account when they consider the overall financing of all forms they are prepared to offer you, and any security and personal guarantees taken for other facilities will also secure balances on the business card.

Government Loan Guarantee Scheme

The Small Firms Loan Guarantee Scheme (to give its full title) is a scheme whereby the Department of Trade and Industry provides the bank with a guarantee should your business not be able to service the loan.

It is intended to assist small businesses to raise money from the banks in cases where:

- The bank considers the business to be viable.
- Adequate security is not available.

The scheme may not be available to enable you to buy an existing business. However, it could be available if you need money later to finance expansion or the purchase of additional assets.

It sounds great, but remember this:

- Before you can obtain the DTI guarantee you must secure the loan with any security you have available – in other words, you could not use the scheme to avoid risking security, such as your home, that you are not keen to offer.
- You must convince the bank that your project is viable, as for any other lending.
- Although the interest rate charged by the bank, due to the DTI guarantee, is competitive, there is a guarantee fee to be paid to the DTI in addition. This means it is expensive money.

The general loan terms are currently as follows:

LENDERS

The scheme is operated by the high street banks.

AMOUNT

For new businesses, or businesses up to two years old, the maximum loan is £100,000. For businesses established longer, up to £250,000 can be made available.

LOAN PERIOD

For two to ten years.

INTEREST

Fixed or variable rates available, the latter typically 2 per cent over bank base rate.

GUARANTEE FEE

Two per cent per annum on the outstanding balance of the loan.

ARRANGEMENT FEE

One per cent payable at outset.

For further information you will need to speak to your business advisor or your local business banker at the high street bank of your choice.

Invoice finance (factoring)

Invoice finance, or factoring, is a means of raising cash against unpaid invoices you have issued to your customers for goods and services supplied on credit terms.

It is more than just a form of raising finance for your business. There are three aspects to the service that you can use, according to need:

- To raise finance against your customers' unpaid invoices.
- Credit management.
- Credit insurance.

Raising finance

When you issue an invoice to a customer you send a copy to the factoring company. The factoring company will advance an agreed percentage of the invoice amount, typically 70–85 per cent.

The customer is advised that the invoice has been assigned to the factoring company and that payment must be made to them, not to you. When the customer pays, the factoring company sends you the balance of the invoice amount.

Credit administration

The factoring company maintains records of the outstanding invoices and undertakes the task of chasing for payment, sending you reports on a regular basis, and freeing you from utilising valuable time on this most boring and unpleasant of tasks.

Credit protection

The factoring company is able to check out the credit standing of your clients and set credit limits for each one. This can normally be done very quickly using Internet-based systems to which you would not have direct access yourself.

Credit insurance can be arranged to protect you against losses due to bad debts.

What types of businesses qualify?

Factoring is generally suitable for businesses selling locally or abroad, on credit terms, with a turnover of at least £100,000 per annum from such activities.

In view of the high set-up costs, factoring companies are not normally interested in businesses with a lower turnover than this. Equally, smaller businesses would not find the financing and credit administration services cost effective anyway, although protection against bad debts through credit insurance is always worth considering and can be arranged, if necessary through other sources.

How much does it all cost?

FINANCE

Interest is charged from the date the advance is made against the invoice until the customer pays. The rate is similar to overdraft rates (typically 2 to 5 per cent above base rate depending on your status).

CREDIT ADMINISTRATION

Typically up to 3 per cent of value of invoices factored, i.e. total invoice values, not the percentage that has been advanced.

CREDIT PROTECTION

Typically 0.5 per cent of total invoice values.

As you can see, whilst the interest charge for money borrowed is similar to overdraft or term loan rates, the overall cost of factoring could be as much as 6 per cent or more of sales if all the services are taken. However, the cost must be weighed against the benefits in taking advantage of the administration skills, credit checking and protection service offered, not to mention the saving of your time and possibly wage costs for employees to do the work.

Sources of factoring services

All the high street banks have factoring subsidiaries, and there are numerous independents as well.

The independents often advance higher percentages of the invoice amounts than do the factoring arms of the high street banks. However, do bear in mind that if you factor with anyone, especially an independent, you are removing the debtors as available security for any general overdraft facility you may require. Since a well spread portfolio of debtors is generally regarded as one of the more attractive forms of security, you should consider discussing the likely impact on any overdraft limit you may be negotiating before committing to go down the factoring route.

Vehicle finance

It is beyond the remit of this book to include detailed information on the various vehicle finance schemes available. However, the following general pointers can be offered for the business owner/ owner-to-be:

Types

The options available to businesses are similar to those available to individuals:

CONTRACT HIRE

Under contract hire you pay a fixed hire cost to include all maintenance. You never own the car, but simply pay the monthly fee, send it for regular maintenance, and hand it back at the end of the contract period. The contract period will normally be a minimum of two years, up to a maximum of four years. Applies to new vehicles only.

CONTRACT PURCHASE

Very similar to contract hire, except legal title is transferred into the business name when all the payments are made, unless you elect to hand the vehicle back at a pre-agreed resale price. The contract period is normally a minimum of two years, up to a maximum four years.

HIRE PURCHASE

New or second-hand vehicles.

SALE AND LEASEBACK

Useful if you are taking over a business with existing vehicles that are already owned.

The choice as to whether to take one of these options, or whether simply to include the vehicles in any general term loans or overdraft being arranged will depend on two factors:

TAX

You will need to get your accountant to advise you which is the most tax efficient for you. If the vehicle is being solely used for business purposes (a delivery lorry, for example) the contract hire and contract purchase schemes are fully tax deductible and therefore very tax efficient for most. If an element of private use comes into it on the other hand, it will be much more complex to work out. It all depends on individual circumstances.

RESOURCES

If you are looking for a sizeable overall funding to acquire and run the business, it is often wise to use specialised finance whenever possible so that the request for general funding can be kept down as much as possible.

Purchasing power

One of the advantages of arranging vehicle finance for new vehicles can be the greater purchasing power available to the financial institution.

Fleets

Many of the banks and finance houses have special schemes where a fleet of vehicles is involved.

Sources of vehicle finance

When you buy a vehicle from a dealer, the salesman is always able to offer you the in-house finance deal. However, it is always worth taking a look at alternatives since there are so many finance institutions offering vehicle finance these days. Many are cheaper and better than you will be offered at the garage.

Commercial mortgages

Commercial mortgages, as the name implies, are available for purchasers of businesses with freehold or long leasehold properties.

Because they are well secured, commercial mortgages tend to be the cheapest option. As with residential mortgages there is much competition for good business and, as a consequence, a wide variety of schemes.

Typical terms include:

Amount

Up to 70 to 85 per cent of independent valuation. Some lenders will go up to 100 per cent or more if there is additional security, such as goodwill, stock, etc.

Period

Five to 25 years.

Interest rate

Fixed and variable rates are available. Variable rates typically range upwards from 1 per cent over base rate.

Repayment

Many lenders offer flexible repayment terms, such as repayment holidays for two years and soft start (where repayments start low and increase over time).

Insurances

The usual 'key man' and 'critical illness' insurances are normally required. See Chapter 18.

Sources

The high street banks all offer this service, as do a number of independents and other banks. Some independents offer higher percentage advances. However, if you choose a high street bank, the property will be more easily available as security for other facilities, such as an overdraft, from the same bank.

Plant and equipment finance

There are many ways of securing finance for purchases of plant and equipment, most of which have been covered elsewhere.

Term loans

Term loans can be used but, as stated elsewhere, if you are raising a relatively large overall funding amount, it pays to use specialised finance whenever possible.

Asset loans

Similar to term loans, but the plant and equipment is accepted as security. Surprisingly, it is often possible to obtain advances up to a very high percentage of the total cost, although often you will have had to pay for the equipment first. High street banks do offer these facilities, although it may pay to use a broker to find a specialist lender.

Leasing

For acquisitions of plant and equipment, a finance lease is often the most tax-efficient means of financing.

The equipment is owned by the finance company (the 'lessor'), and you (the 'lessee') pay a fixed monthly rental which is normally fully tax deductible.

The typical terms are as follows:

Amount

Up to 100 per cent of the cost can be financed. Most banks and finance houses have a minimum amount, £10,000 being common.

RENTAL RATE

Set at a level to repay fully the capital cost of the asset and interest over the life of the lease agreement. For the interest element, fixed or variable rates are usually available, although for deals up to £25,000 for personal sole trader and partnership businesses a fixed rate may be the only option. Variable rates are set at a percentage over base rate, as for term loans.

VAT

You do not have to pay VAT at the outset because you do not buy the asset. However, rental payments are subject to VAT, which can be reclaimed in the usual way if you are VAT registered. For more information on VAT see Chapter 14.

SECURITY

As the lessor owns the asset, additional security is not normally required, except personal guarantees from the owners of small limited companies.

PERIOD

Three to seven years is normal, although occasionally as short as one year.

TAX

The full rental payments are tax deductible.

AT THE END OF THE TERM

For legal reasons you are not able to buy the asset directly from the lessor. You therefore have two options:

- Extend the lease for a secondary term.
- Arrange on behalf of the leasing company for it to be sold to a third party at fair market value.

If you extend for a further term there will be a nominal annual rental payment. At the end of the secondary term you can return the asset to the lessor or arrange a sale.

Due to legal considerations, whenever you arrange a sale of the asset it must be to a totally unconnected third party. You cannot sell it, for example, to a partner in the business or to a director of the company. Of course, if your best drinking pal buys it with a loan from your wife and lets you borrow it on permanent loan ...

IS LEASING FOR YOU?

As with the choices for vehicle finance, the decision as to whether to take this option, or whether simply to include the asset in any general term loans or overdraft being arranged will depend on two factors: tax and resources.

You will need to get your accountant to advise you which method is the most tax efficient for you.

If you are looking for a sizeable overall funding to acquire and run the business, as already stated earlier, it is often wise to use specialised finance where possible so that the request for general funding can be kept down as much as possible.

Trade creditors

Trade creditors are an important source of finance for many businesses and, if the business you are acquiring enjoys this free source of money, you will want to arrange for this to continue.

However, trade credit for a new business owner may not be easy to arrange, and will certainly take time, so in order to avoid any disruption in supply you need to be doing something about it well before you take over.

It usually works like this. You get an application form from the supplier. The supplier insures his debtors against losses from bad debts, so he sends the form to his insurer for approval. The insurer does a credit check on you and, if you pass muster, notifies a credit limit for you to the supplier.

If you are trading in a sole name or partnership, you will have to supply names and address details, and they can do personal credit checks.

It is sometimes a little trickier if you have formed a new limited company, since you have no personal liability and the company has no track record. You have no trading history, so not unreasonably the credit insurers might be cautious. The initial limit will probably be set quite low, but will be increased as business is successfully transacted.

It is important to remember when you look at your overall financing needs that you may not initially enjoy as much trade credit as the vendor when you first take over, so ensure adequate allowance is made when deciding how much to raise by way of overdraft. As stated earlier, most suppliers will accept business cards so it may be worth including one in the overall facilities you negotiate with your bank.

Raising equity

As you know, having read page 108, an element of the business owner's own money will need to be invested into the business. It is not generally possible, or advisable, to raise 100 per cent by way of debt. Firstly, lenders like to see the business owners being financially committed. But, secondly, the business is likely to suffer if it is burdened with servicing too much debt.

For the vast majority of readers there will only be two ways of raising equity:

- Personal resources.
- Bringing in a business partner.

Bringing in a business partner

If you have insufficient personal resources you will need to find a business partner who is able to introduce capital to make up the shortfall.

If you need help in finding a suitable partner it is worth speaking to your accountant, solicitor or the local *Business Link*.

Bringing in a business partner is certainly a much better solution than borrowing too much, and can be highly successful. However, it can lead to difficulties unless you go about it the right way:

- If it's someone you didn't know before, he could turn out to be problematic or untrustworthy to work with. You will need to investigate him carefully.
- If it's a friend or acquaintance, you know his personality and that he is honest, but going into business together could spoil the relationship.

Either way, it is vitally important to establish the relationship on the right footing from the very beginning.

If it is someone previously unknown to you, get to know him as well as possible before committing to anything, and ask for references from bankers/accountants. If he has been in partnerships before, perhaps you can speak to his partners. If he is offering expertise as well as money, check as far as you can that he can in fact do what he says he can. Do not be embarrassed about asking for these references, because if he objects it means he has something to hide and you should avoid him like the plague. If necessary you can ask him to see your business advisor/accountant and get him to do the checks for you. That way it seems a little less personal but, of course, it will cost you for his time. Whatever you do, DO NOT PROCEED WITHOUT MAKING THESE CHECKS FIRST.

You can enter into the arrangement in the form of a partnership or by forming a limited company (see Chapter 11, page 142, for information on choosing the right business entity). Whichever you choose, you should have a written agreement from the outset.

Partnership agreement

Whether your business partner is a new acquaintance or an old friend, the first step is to write a partnership agreement covering all the key aspects of the relationship. DO THIS BEFORE ANYONE PUTS ANY MONEY IN.

The biggest source of friction in business partnerships arises from a feeling down the road, on the part of one or more of the partners, that they are faced with a situation they hadn't bargained on. This can only arise if there is no written agreement or, where there is one, it doesn't cover the issue causing the friction.

A proper partnership agreement should be prepared by a solicitor. However, so that he can write an agreement that reflects what you have agreed between you, before you see him you will need to discuss and agree how your partnership will work. Prepare a heads of agreement, summarising the main terms. You will be discussing the main terms anyway, so why not write them down, however simplistically, and make a signed copy for each partner and the solicitor? The headings you should cover are these:

AMOUNTS TO BE INVESTED BY EACH PARTNER

PROFIT SHARE FOR EACH PARTNER

This is normally in proportion to the amounts invested, although it might be adjusted where some partners are more active in the business than others. However, where different partners are committing differing amounts of time to the business, I always think that the fairest and easiest way to structure the agreement is so that working partners get a fair salary for time given, and the profit share, to be distributed in proportion to capital invested, is calculated after payment of the salary/salaries.

FUNCTIONS TO BE FULFILLED BY EACH PARTNER

Be as specific as possible. If a partner is not expected to become involved in the running of the business, say so.

TIME COMMITMENT TO BE GIVEN TO THE BUSINESS BY EACH ACTIVE PARTNER

SALARIES AND EXPENSES, AND DRAWINGS

Take trouble over this one, as partners can become very niggled when they think one of the other partners is drawing too much for salary and expenses, leaving lower profits for distribution. Stipulate a salary for each active partner according to time commitment and a reasonable rate for the job. Stipulate what car expenses can be drawn (a fixed rate for business mileage is probably the easiest answer, because then it's down to the individual whether he spends his personal money on a Mercedes rather than a Reliant Robin).

LENGTH OF COMMITMENT

I always feel it is a good idea to state in this heads of agreement that the partnership is expected to endure for a minimum time, just to show that the intention was not for a short-term temporary relationship. The last thing you want is to find that a year down the road your partner finds another use for the money and wants to pull out, leaving you with no option but to sell the business.

If, on the other hand, you hope it is temporary and you would like to pay your partner out as soon as you can so that the business is yours alone, state this fact in the heads of agreement. If you are doing well he might not be keen to go when the time comes, unless this agreement clearly shows that that is what he always knew to be the intention, and agreed to it.

TERMINATION OF PARTNERSHIP

It is usual for a notice period to be given when a partner wishes to withdraw, and for the other partners to be offered first option to buy out his share(s) at a fair market price. To establish a fair price it is usual to have a valuation carried out, either by the partnership accountant or someone else similarly qualified and suitably independent.

BANK MANDATES

The agreement should stipulate how the bank account will be set up, in particular the signing arrangements.

Needing two signatures on every cheque is generally cumbersome in practice, but the agreement should stipulate the threshold above which all cheques need two signatures.

A little word of warning here – these days the banks rarely check signatures, so don't rely on them to pick up the fact that a partner is issuing cheques on a single signature when he shouldn't.

You can only sue the bank for actual losses suffered. If the partner has a night on the town out of business funds, you just might have a claim against the bank. However, if the partner bought an expensive computer for the business which you would not have approved had you known, the business has the computer so there is no loss, and thus no liability on the bank.

PARTNERSHIP MEETINGS/MANAGEMENT POWERS

The agreement should state the frequency of partners' meetings. It should also state what decisions need to be agreed by all partners before going ahead (the purchase of the above computer, for example). Usually the agreement stipulates an amount above which approval from all partners is needed for purchases of a capital nature.

ACCOUNTING

The agreement should stipulate the firm of accountants who are to be appointed to audit the books.

This list is by no means exhaustive, but if you use it as an agenda you will find yourselves covering most of the important issues.

Professional investors

There is a wide variety of professional investors, such as venture capital companies, development agencies and business angels (wealthy individuals). They are all looking for two things:

- Exceptional returns on their investments.
- An exit route within about five years.

These sources are not available for the run-of-the-mill business purchase. However, if you feel they could be relevant to you, go along to your local *Business Link* who can advise you and, where appropriate, will be able to effect introductions to possible investors.

Chapter 11:

Choosing a Legal Entity for Your Business

There are three types of legal entity that can be used for running your business:

- Sole trader.
- Partnership.
- Limited company.

In the following paragraphs you will find a brief description of the three alternatives. The notes are not comprehensive, but cover the main considerations to be taken into account when deciding which to choose. Read about all three before making a final decision.

For the sake of completeness, mention should be made at this point of two specialised legal entities – companies limited by guarantee and limited partnerships. However, these are not generally used in small trading businesses and are not, therefore, covered in this book.

The references to 'debts' in the following paragraphs do not just mean loans, but cover all business liabilities – loans, overdrafts, trade credit, tax, VAT, etc.

Sole trader

As the name implies, this business format can only be used if you are trading as a single owner in your own name. In legal terms, the business does not exist as a separate entity – you and the business are one and the same. In financial terms, you are fully responsible for all business debts as it is you personally who has incurred the liability.

The bank account will be called something like 'John Smith trading as Pilem High Gadgets'.

To comply with law, all important business documents, such as headed notepaper and invoices, must give details of the business owner if a trading name is used. In the above example it would not be sufficient to simply state 'Pilem High Gadgets' and the address. It would have to be made clear, usually as a footer, that it is John Smith trading under that name.

If you are leaving paid employment to go into business there are often tax advantages in the early years to being a sole trader, particularly if you expect not to make an immediate profit (you may be able to claim back some of the tax that had been deducted by your former employer from your pay). However check with your accountant, and read about limited companies below before making your final decision, as tax is not the only consideration.

Partnership

A partnership is a legally defined term. Partnerships are governed by the various Partnership Acts and by some aspects of the Companies Acts. These Acts do not affect you on a day-to-day basis, so they are nothing to worry about, but they will affect how your solicitor writes the partnership agreement, and how your accountant prepares the annual accounts.

If there are two or more of you, you need to decide whether to be a partnership or a limited company.

All partners are fully liable for the debts of the partnership, in the same way as a sole trader. In normal circumstances, you cannot get out of liability by claiming that the other partner was not authorised to incur the debt.

As with a sole trader, all important documents such as invoices must give details of ownership if a trading name is used – i.e. any name that does not include all the partners' full names. Some partnerships, such as large firms of solicitors for example, have many partners, and putting all the names on the stationery would be impractical. Therefore, the law states that either all the part-ners' names must be shown or a statement as to where their details can be seen must be included.

If you could trade as a sole trader, the alternative of forming a partnership with your spouse/partner might be suggested by your accountant, as he may feel it would be advantageous to split the income for tax purposes. The problem with this is that, as a partner, the spouse/partner then becomes liable for the business debts. A better solution might be to take the spouse/partner on as an employee and pay a salary. That would certainly provide better protection for the family home (unless it has been offered to a lender as security, of course).

You will need to have a partnership agreement drawn up. This is covered on page 138.

Limited company

A limited company is a separate legal entity in its own right. The term 'limited' in this context means that the shareholders' liability is limited to the share capital they invested. In other words, if you bought some shares in Tesco's and they went bust (some chance!), you lose your investment, but you cannot be asked to contribute any more to pay off Tesco's creditors.

A limited company is owned by its shareholders and run by its directors. There must be at least two shareholders, but there can be a single director. The company is registered at the appropriate Companies House, has a registered number, and has an official address which is called the 'Registered Office'. All formal documents served on the company must be served at the Registered Office to be validly served.

All important documents must state the company name in full, where (country) the company is registered, the registered number and the address of the Registered Office.

Forming a limited company is the only way that you can limit in any way your personal liability for business debts. It sounds ideal, but there are other considerations, both pluses and minuses:

- A new company has no track record on which to base credit decisions. Therefore financial institutions will almost invariably insist on personal guarantees from the shareholders. Creditors, such as trade creditors, who are not able to take guarantees may not initially be prepared to sell on credit.
- A limited company is not a licence to act irresponsibly. Directors can be made personally liable if they do not run the company's business in a financially responsible manner.
- Anyone who has a strong influence over the way the company is run will be regarded as a director, even if he is not

formally appointed as one (this is called being a 'shadow director'), and as such he could become personally liable for company debts in the event of financial irresponsibility in the company's affairs.

- The above provisions are clearly designed to stop reckless people hiding behind a limited company. That said, we have all seen examples on the television where people get away with it, and it does happen all the time with small businesses.

- The limited company gives your accountant more options on how you are paid – by salary or by dividend – which may help your tax and National Insurance situation. There are also more options for pension arrangements.

- The other important consideration is when stock is to be used as security for a bank debt. In order to have effective security over stock, a bank needs to take what is called a 'floating charge'.

  A legal 'charge' is a term to describe taking security over something. For example, if you have taken a mortgage to buy your house, the mortgage is a legal charge over the house. In the case of your house, it is called a fixed charge because the house doesn't change. You are not allowed to sell it without accounting to the mortgage lender.

  If a charge is taken over stock in a business, the individual stock items come and go on a daily basis and, unless you are given permission to buy and sell in the ordinary course of trading, you clearly could not run the business. The bank takes a 'floating' charge whereby it is secured by whatever items of stock are there at any given time, and you are allowed to buy and sell as long as it is in the normal course of trading.

  A limited company is the only business entity that can give such security so, if you are acquiring a business where the value of stock is substantial and will need to be used to secure finance, a limited company could be your only option.

A limited company is easily formed. Your accountant/solicitor can arrange it for you, or you can go directly to one of the specialist company formation agents (why not do the latter – it is simple and may save you money on accountants'/solicitors' charges?). Formation agents are usually based in offices near the registry (Cardiff, for example, for companies to be formed in England and Wales) or in other major cities. They advertise in *Yellow Pages*, as well as the business-to-business sections of national and regional newspapers. Fees are fairly standard, and it should not cost you much more than £100 or so to form a company.

Forming a limited company can be a good way to go into business with a partner, since the limited liability aspect might protect you and your personal assets if your partner does something financially rash. Although it is not a partnership as such, if you are forming a limited company with a business partner it is a good idea to draw up an agreement similar to a partnership agreement. In this case you would call it a shareholders' agreement, but you would cover the same general headings as described already for a partnership agreement (see page 138).

What if the business is already trading as a limited company?

If the vendor is already trading as a limited company he may suggest you take the company over. This is very easy to do because all you need to do is execute a deed of transfer in respect of the shares. Since the business is owned by the company, and you now own the company, you now own the business. However, this is not generally a good idea because, however careful your investigation, you can never be certain that some unexpected creditors might not turn up with financial claims on the company at a later date. It is far better to start with a brand-new company with no history.

Chapter 12:

Arranging Contracts

Unless the transaction is very small you will need to appoint a solicitor to act for you, in very much the same way as for buying a house.

Very small transactions

With very small transactions a solicitor's fees could add a disproportional amount to the cost of acquiring the business. Very occasionally, in these circumstances, the business transfer agent will agree to act as an independent facilitator for the parties. The sale price would need to be small, up to an absolute maximum of £10,000, and the transaction very simple – possibly something like a low-key cleaning service or mail order business operated from home. There would need to be no property purchase or lease involved, or indeed any major assets at all, and the terms between buyer and seller would have to be very straightforward.

If you think your transaction falls into this category, and you do not feel able to do it all yourself, it may be worth asking the business transfer agent if he is willing to undertake this for you before approaching a solicitor.

Appointing a solicitor

Solicitors are like many other professionals – there are horses for courses. A firm that is excellent for divorces or wills may have no experience with business transactions, and it is therefore important to ensure that the firm you appoint has the necessary expertise.

Although ultimately you are always protected by the Law Society against losses suffered due to the negligence or dishonesty of a solicitor, buying a business can be legally quite complex, so you need more than just that comfort. A good solicitor will ask all the right questions of the other side, will give you the best protection in the contract with the vendor (which will often be more complex than the standard one for buying a house) and will be able to give you good advice throughout the progress of the transaction. If he is commercially aware, he will be able to advise you on any detailed negotiation points with the vendor that arise during this stage – for example, what is included in the contract with respect to acquisition of stock (see Chapter 13).

Therefore you need to ensure that you appoint a solicitor who has the right experience. If you do not know such a firm yourself, ask friends or relatives who own businesses, or ask the business transfer agent for a recommendation.

Make sure that the solicitor is aware of any valuation report or survey that you or your lender have had commissioned, and that he gets copies so that he can ensure that any recommendations for further reports or enquiries are carried out.

Contractual terms

You will need to discuss with the solicitor the conditions that you have agreed with the vendor so that he can include them in the legal contract.

Chapter 13:

Paying for Stock and Debtors

PAYING FOR STOCK

Stock is changing on a day-by-day basis, so it is normally paid for separately on the day of takeover when it is normal to bring in an independent firm of stocktakers to do a full stock take and calculate value.

Stocktakers

Stocktakers have their special systems for doing this job very fast, so unless it is the type of business that does not carry much in the way of stock don't try to do it yourself.

Sometimes the vendor and purchaser each appoint his own firm, and the two firms get together to agree a figure between them. However, in many cases this is an unnecessary duplication of expense and it is often easiest to use the firm that the vendor has used in the past to act for both sides. You can then split the cost.

Provided they are a reputable firm, and most are, this is not as risky as it sounds. Firstly, having undertaken stock checks in the past at this particular business they are very familiar with it, and can reach an accurate figure much quicker than a new firm would probably do. Secondly, they are at least as keen to impress you, the buyer, as they are to please the seller, because he is leaving and they will be hoping to retain the business after you take over. In any event, as a reputable firm, they would not certify a stock figure they were not happy with in any circumstances.

What to exclude

You need to agree with the vendor what stock you are prepared to take over and pay for. Just because it's on the shelf doesn't mean you have to pay for it.

149

If in discussions with the vendor it has become clear that certain lines or products have not been a success, tell him you don't intend to pay for that stock, or at least negotiate a reduced price so that you can afford to put it on sale at an irresistible sale price.

With most retail businesses you should put a limit on the age of stock that you will buy. In the case of food, it obviously has to be fresh. In the case of toys, maybe 90 days is reasonable. In the case of greetings cards, you would not want to pay for the leftovers of last year's Christmas, Mother's Day or other seasons. You will need to consider what is reasonable for the particular type of business you are buying.

Invoices

If the stock consists of items that could be faulty and need to be returned, make sure that you have details of suppliers, and preferably copies of the previous owner's account numbers and invoices.

Settling up

The completion of the purchase of the business is settled between the solicitors.

However, because of the last-minute nature, stock is usually paid for by way of cheque handed over directly to the vendor on the day.

PAYING FOR DEBTORS

The simple rule here is don't. What if you pay the vendor and then the debtor defaults?

The vendor should give you a list of outstanding debtors as at completion and should write to the debtors to notify them that all debts up to the completion date are payable to him, and any subsequent invoices to you. Obviously you can send on any cheques you receive for him.

In Chapter 10, which deals with financing your business, we covered the possibility of raising working capital by factoring the debtors. If the vendor has factored the debtors, then the issue will not arise in quite this way, as the debtors will pay the amounts to the factoring company who will then account to the vendor.

If you decide to use factoring as a part of your finance you may find it advantageous to use the current factoring house, since they will already have set up limits for the existing clients of the business. It is highly likely that the vendor will put this to you, possibly being helpful, but possibly also thinking that if you take over the factoring agreements he will collect his money and be off the hook as far as any possible comeback is concerned.

However, the factoring house will consider any deal with you as a brand-new arrangement, so if you agree that you will take over the factoring from the vendor they will make a new advance to you, and you will pay him. There seems no point in doing that. What do you gain? If a debtor defaults, you will suffer whatever clawback may be claimed by the factoring house, whilst the vendor, who has made the profit on the original sale, gets off free and clear. It is much better to agree that the vendor gets the money when, and only when, the debtor pays. As the new owner you have no possible advantage in it being any other way.

In any event, before continuing the arrangement with the present factoring house, you will need to look at alternatives to ensure that the vendor had a good deal. The fact that the factoring house had limits already set up is not a very persuasive argument because a new factoring house, given the client list, could organise limits very quickly.

Chapter 14:

VAT – an Overview

Value Added Tax is a very wide subject which, in its detailed implementation, affects different businesses in different ways. It is not, therefore, possible to present a complete guide here and you should take expert advice, normally from your accountant, to check how it applies in your case. However, the basic system is always the same, and the following is an overview of the general principles which will give you a good understanding of how it works.

Once you have sorted out how it applies to your business, and you have organised a system of record keeping to deal with it, VAT should not be a problem to administer. All the leading accounting software handles VAT accounting records automatically, and there are many helpful sources of advice to make sure you do it correctly right from the start.

VAT is administered by HM Revenue & Customs (referred to herein as HMRC for short). How VAT affects you, and whether you can or must register with HMRC for VAT, will primarily be dependent on the goods and/or services you supply, and the amount of your turnover. More detailed information, including basic publications to get you started, can be obtained on their website (see Appendix 4).

What goods and services are subject to VAT?

All goods and services are potentially subject to VAT, but for VAT calculation purposes there are four categories:

- Standard rated.
- Reduced rate.
- Zero rated.
- Exempt.

Standard rated

The vast majority of goods and services are standard rated. This means that VAT is charged at the current standard rate announced by the Chancellor of the Exchequer. At the time of writing the standard rate is 17.5 per cent, which has been unchanged for a number of years.

Reduced rate

A very few items, domestic fuel for example, are charged at a reduced rate, which at the time of writing is 5 per cent.

Zero rated

Some goods and services are subject to VAT, but the rate is set at 0 per cent. These goods and services could become subject to the standard rate at any time the Chancellor decides to change their status. Children's clothes are an example.

Exempt

The exempt category includes a relatively short list of goods and services which are very unlikely ever to be subject to VAT. Examples include residential care and nursing home fees, insurance premiums and medicines.

Who should register for VAT?

Businesses whose turnover is solely derived from supplying exempt goods and services cannot register, even if they want to. All other businesses either can or must register.

Any business that is registered must add VAT at the appropriate rate to invoices for goods and services. Businesses not registered must not add VAT to invoices.

Any business supplying goods and services in the standard rated or zero rated categories, with a turnover above the registration threshold must register. The threshold is normally reviewed annually and any changes are announced in the Chancellor's annual budget. Check the HMRC website or telephone helpline for the up-to-date threshold. Businesses below the limit can elect to register if they so wish.

In summary:

- A nursing home cannot register under any circumstances.
- A cleaning business (cleaning services are standard rated) turning over £30,000 per annum can choose to register if it so wishes, but must add VAT to its charges if it does.
- A cleaning business turning over £150,000 per annum must by law register and must charge VAT.

The natural question to ask here is how does the £30,000 cleaning business decide whether or not to register? In order to be able to answer that question logically it is necessary first to explain how VAT is accounted for.

Accounting for VAT

This is done by returns submitted periodically to HMRC along with whatever payment is due. The standard period for a return is quarterly, but HMRC do allow different reporting periods (see comments later).

Any business which is registered must charge its customers the appropriate VAT (the standard, reduced or zero rate) as already stated. But the *quid pro quo* is that it can reclaim VAT paid on invoices for expenses, which an unregistered business cannot do.

Let's take our £30,000 cleaning company as an example and let's assume it has elected to register. Because it is registered, it will have invoiced its customers a total of £35,250, being £30,000 plus VAT at 17.5 per cent.

To keep it simple, other than wages which are not covered by VAT, we will assume that the only other expenses were cleaning materials amounting to £11,750 (which included £1,750 VAT charged by the supplier at the standard rate).

The VAT return would look like this:

VAT charged on sales in the period	£5,250
VAT paid on expenses in the period	£1,750
Net VAT payable to HMRC	£3,500

The return would be sent, along with a cheque for £3,500, to HMRC.

The VAT exercise does not mean that the business will have to pay extra in any way because the transactions are in balance:

Amounts received

From VAT added to customer invoices	£5,250

Amounts paid

Net paid with VAT return	£3,500
Paid on expense invoices	£1,750
	£5,250

Indeed, since the customers paid their £5,250 to you before your settlement with HMRC you have actually had the benefit of £3,500 of the money in your bank account for a while.

The other benefit to the business has been the ability to reclaim the £1,750 paid in VAT on the invoices for materials by deducting it from the amount paid to HMRC.

Considerations for voluntary registration

As already stated, if you are a nursing home or other business with turnover entirely comprising exempt goods and services, you cannot register in any circumstances. Other businesses above the threshold must register.

For other businesses below the threshold, as you will have appreciated by now, all other things being equal, a business is more profitable (by the amount of VAT reclaimed) if it registers. The cleaning company used in our example has a net turnover of £30,000, registered or not. But if it is registered, its net expenses would be £10,000, whereas as an unregistered business it would not have been able to reclaim the VAT and the materials would have cost it £11,750.

Another possible matter to check is the lease on the premises, if there is one. Some landlords charge VAT on rent and some don't (the reasons for this are outside the scope of this book). The savings by reclaiming VAT on rent might be substantial.

So, it seems pretty obvious that registration is beneficial. There are just two possible downsides to consider as well:

The effect on your customers

If your customers are VAT-registered they will be able to reclaim any VAT you charge, so they will not be unduly concerned if you register and suddenly your invoices are larger. However, if they are not able to reclaim the VAT you will increase their expenses.

To take the example of the cleaning business again, if their business is cleaning offices their customers will almost certainly be registered for VAT, and registering would not adversely affect the business. But if it is a domestic cleaning business, the customers will be private individuals who may cancel rather than be faced with paying extra.

In the latter case, the loss of customers may be greater than the saving on expenses.

The extra record keeping

Once you are registered you will need to keep VAT records. But this is not normally a big task once you have a system set up and, as already stated, computer accounts programs do the maths for you.

Even if the accounting for VAT frightens you, calculate the savings to be made on expenses, and consider whether it may be beneficial to employ a bookkeeper for a few hours a week.

Taking over from the previous owner

If the existing owner is already VAT registered, you can either apply to take over his registration or you can apply for a new registration in your name. It is always advisable to start a new registration in case there is any 'baggage' with the old one.

If the business is registered voluntarily, and you have concluded that you prefer not to register, there is no need to do so. The only difference is that as you are not registered the vendor will have to charge you VAT for any goods he sells to you that are subject to VAT. This would include VAT on any stock and assets you are taking over, as well as the price for the goodwill, and which could add substantially to the amount you will need to pay over at completion. It might pay to register for VAT for at least a while to be able to avoid such VAT being added to the business purchase costs, but you should take your accountant's advice on this.

Getting advice

Accountants are the normal source of advice on VAT matters and should be consulted if necessary about whether or not to register.

Once you have decided to register you will find HMRC very helpful in putting you on the right road, including visits to look at the record and accounting systems you are planning to use, and giving advice as to whether the systems are adequate and correctly based.

Chapter 15:

Presentation and Marketing of the Business

Any new business will take a year to reach its full potential from a running start, and an established business needs a lot of *TLC* to effect a smooth changeover.

So, before you take the reins, make sure you have budgeted adequately for marketing and promotion as a very real expense in the first twelve months.

How you elect to market your business depends very much on what you are selling – a commodity or a service. But the basics are still the same: to put your business in the face of all your potential customers and make it stand out from the rest.

Ask the vendor

You can't ask too many questions before embarking in business. If you're buying an existing business, ask the vendor how he does his marketing and what return he gets from, say, advertising in the local papers. Ask to see invoices for expenditure on advertising. If it's a shop, then wander round surrounding shops and chat to other shopkeepers and their customers. Get the feel for how they perceive your prospective business – do they even know it's there?! It's amazing how you can walk past a shop, let's say a locksmith, and never notice it because you don't need a new lock. But when suddenly your key breaks in the front door and you need one immediately, do you know where to find one? The local locksmith who has done the presentation of his business the best is likely to be the one you will think of first.

Retail businesses

If your business is a shop or post office, you are probably going to be in a high street or precinct and depend very much on passing trade and regular customers. So you have to tempt in customers with attractive window dressing, special offers and sell yourself as a friendly, helpful trader whom people trust and enjoy visiting.

It is very difficult to make the general public see anything new. You will be amazed how many people will ask where the toys are, despite your having put up a large sign! Or if it's a new line they will say, as they suddenly see the toys on the way to something else in the shop, 'I didn't know you sold toys – I went all the way to the next town yesterday to buy some.' That was despite a sign outside for the past two months advertising that you now sell them. You will have to be very creative to ensure that people notice what you are doing.

At the same time these days, people are used to shopping in nice environments and will quickly be put off from coming in if the shop is looking old-fashioned or tired and in need of a refurbishment. It is very important to keep the shop looking as smart as possible, especially if food is involved.

Do spend at least a little money on a coat of paint if it needs it. If the shop has been green for the past 60 years, why not paint it bright blue? It would be a very good way to get it noticed and create interest in the fact that it has new owners.

Service businesses

If your business does not rely on footfall past your door, you must still make people very aware of your existence.

Therefore marketing is an essential tool of absolutely every such business at some level. The vendor of the business will know what has worked well in the past and, just as importantly, what didn't. If there were a magic formula for marketing it would have been patented years ago, but the truth is there isn't one. It is very difficult to know in advance what will work and what will simply fail to produce results. Trial and error is often the only way, so be reluctant to change what the vendor has been successfully doing up to now.

We will explore a few ideas you can apply to get your new venture or diversification off to a flying start.

Identify your potential customers

Who are they? It is absolutely essential to identify the people or other businesses that are going to need your services. For example, if your new business is a contract cleaning business you know your customers are going to be other commercial businesses and they are not passing trade. You have to find them at a time when they need a new cleaning contract.

If you elect to run a dating agency you have to find ways of tempting single people to trust you to find them their perfect partner – an altogether more delicate and personal approach is required.

The approaches in these two examples clearly need to be quite different. The cleaning company needs to target marketing in a way that emphasises what makes a cleaning company attractive to potential clients. It will need to consider what are the most frequent complaints that clients have about their cleaners, and concentrate the marketing towards convincing prospects that they will not have these problems in the future if they change over. The dating agency, on the other hand, will need to think about all the natural fears that people will have in using such a service, and allay them.

Even if you are taking over a successful business where the marketing seems to have been good, consider the special issues that apply to your new business and think about whether the marketing could be beneficially tweaked in some ways.

Advertising

Many entrepreneurs begin by placing advertisements in their local or national papers and wonder why it doesn't work very well. They may get the odd call or customer, but may have spent hundreds of pounds for a return of very little.

When you look through your newspaper, what catches your eye in an advert? Is it size, colour, content or the fact that it has Special Offer plastered all over it? Or if you are honest, do you barely glance at the display adverts and go on to read the news items?

Advertising is an essential income for any newspaper and they will try to sell you space, promising the earth as soon as they spot you are new in the neighbourhood. Representatives come and visit offering special rates if you buy so many column centimetres a week for several weeks and you can be tempted into spending your entire budget.

If you want to try a few adverts, take the initiative. Call the paper and ask for late space – that is anything they have left shortly before their deadline. They will usually offer you a 50 per cent discount straightaway. Don't take it! Offer them a really low amount and often a compromise can be reached at perhaps 30 per cent of the original cost.

Always try to get your advert on a right-hand page. If you imagine reading a paper on your lap, it is always easier to read the right-hand page and the nearer the front of the paper the better.

You can waste a lot of money on advertising. Advertising in most minor publications will not work. Opportunities like advertising on the surrounds of local maps, or business cards in dispensers in DIY chains, simply do not work. It is very easy for the salesman to quote how many thousands of people visit the DIY store or use the maps, but the fact is that nobody will notice your advertisement or business card.

At the same time, bear in mind that advertising tends to work better the more it is repeated. People will often not react until they have seen your advertisement two or three times. Therefore, if you do decide to try an advertisement in the local paper do not expect miracles in the first week, and give it at least a three- or four-week trial before you decide if it is worthwhile. You may find you can get a better deal from the publication by booking a run.

Sell the benefits, not the features

There is little point in putting any advertisement anywhere unless it contains a useful message. This applies to posters, handbills and fliers, as well as advertisements in publications.

You must sell the BENEFITS of your product not the features. Look at any professional advert and you will see it promotes what the product can do for you. The fact that it is bright green, smells nice or attracts mice is irrelevant. The important points would be that it made acne vanish, took six inches off your hips instantly or provided a life-saving service. Use the words 'you' and 'your' frequently in the advert thus:

> *Your local computer shop, here when you need us.*
> *Put yourself in our hands – then relax.*

Perhaps the most famous by-line was coined by L'Oréal which they use for all their products and it says so much:

> *Because you're worth it.*

Internet

These days it is not expensive to have a simple website designed and hosted, and it is almost a marketing 'must'. By referring to a website in your advertisements you can direct people to the site where you can provide far more information than you ever could in an advertisement.

Increasingly people are communicating by e-mail because it is so quick and flexible. If your business is called 'Rent-a-villa' it looks so much more professional if your e-mail address is *sales@rent-a-villa.co.uk* rather than *smith2348@yahoo.com*. You can register your own domain to enable you to do this, as well as have *www.rent-a-villa.co.uk* as your website for less than £100 per year. This would be money very well spent for most service businesses.

Networking

Particularly if your new business is a business-to-business service you will find it very worthwhile joining the local business clubs such as The Chamber of Commerce and the Business Breakfast Club. Word of mouth is by far the best, and cheapest, form of marketing.

Chapter 16:

Employing Staff

There are libraries full of books on this subject, so necessarily this can only be a quick guide to get you started.

Whilst employment law is growing ever more complex, it is not a huge headache for most small businesses, particularly if approached sensibly.

Existing staff

When you buy a business, whether you like it or not, the staff employed on the day you take over come with it, along with all the employees' rights they enjoyed with the previous owner, such as wages, holidays, notice periods, redundancy rights and so forth. That is their right in law so, if you know someone is not up to the job, try to get the vendor to deal with him before you take over.

If the business is currently run through a limited company and you are buying that company you simply continue the existing PAYE scheme. Otherwise, the vendor must give you a P45 for each employee which notifies the Inland Revenue of the change of employer.

PAYE scheme

Unless you are continuing an existing company scheme (as referred to in the preceding paragraph) you will need to open a new PAYE scheme with the Inland Revenue. They will send you a pack with all the rules on record keeping, tax tables, etc., and they do have helplines you can refer to.

You will be expected to deduct tax in accordance with the employees' tax codes, as well as national insurance, and pay these sums over to the Inland Revenue at least quarterly.

Computer programs

Many of the leading accounts programs, including QuickBooks and Sage, have utilities to manage the payroll for you. It usually involves paying an annual fee, and you need an Internet connection so that the program can keep the tax tables and NI contribution books up to date. All you need to do is set up the employees' details and amend tax coding details when you receive notifications of changes from the Inland Revenue. Each time you put in gross pay, the program will do the calculations so you can print off pay slips, and it will post all the necessary bookkeeping entries into your accounts.

Payroll services

If you are new to running a business, and have no previous experience with payroll, it may be a good idea to engage a payroll service to do it for you. It is not usually very expensive and will save you valuable time in the early days when you will have a lot more important issues to get to grips with. Most firms of accountants and many employment agencies provide a payroll service. You just give them the details of gross pay each week or month, and they do the calculations, keep the records, and produce the pay slips.

Pension scheme

Under the Government's latest pension rules, any business employing five or more (including the owner), must offer its workers an option to take out a stakeholder pension scheme. Although the business does not have to contribute, it does have the obligation to make a scheme available by way of deduction from pay. Your accountant will be able to introduce you to a specialist who can look after this for you.

New employees

However much you like someone, always take written references from previous employers unless it is a first job, in which case you will need school or personal references.

Staff handbook and contracts of employment

If you are a business with more than one or two employees, you should have a staff handbook which sets out rules on dress code, smoking, timekeeping and so on, and covers procedures for issuing verbal and written warnings and dismissal. It should also set out a complaints procedure for employees.

Similarly, all employees should be given a simple form of contract, setting out basic terms of employment such as pay and holiday entitlement, notice period, pay days, and stating that the employee agrees to abide by the staff handbook, a copy of which each acknowledges he has received.

This may sound pedantic, but it takes little effort to write in the early days, and will solve a lot of problems and wasted time in the event of disputes with employees later on, if, for example, you fire someone and he thinks it is unfair. If you have a dispute with an employee, he can take his grievance to an employment tribunal. Tribunals always ask what handbooks there are, and whether normal procedures have been followed. If you have a handbook, and always follow it rigidly, it is likely that an employee will be advised he has no case worth taking to tribunal.

Indeed The Employment Rights Act 1996 requires employers to provide most employees, within two calendar months of starting work, with a written statement of the main terms of the contract. Department of Trade and Industry leaflets PL700 and PL700A cover these issues.

You don't need to write these documents from scratch – many books on employment include samples, and your local *Business Link* will have something in the library. The ACAS website (see Appendix 4) also has some very useful examples and general publications.

The following details must be included in the contract of employment and handbook:

- The employer's name.
- The employee's name.
- The job title or a brief job description.
- The date employment began, the place of work and the address of the employer.
- The amount of pay and the interval between payments.
- Hours of work.
- Holiday pay entitlement.

- Sick pay arrangements.
- Pension arrangements.
- Notice periods.
- Where the employment is not permanent, the period it is expected to continue.
- Where the employment is for a fixed term, the date when it is to end.
- Grievance and appeal arrangements.
- Disciplinary rules
- Any collective agreements which directly affect the terms and conditions.

Chapter 17:

Bookkeeping and Audit

The dreaded accounts have to be done, I'm afraid, and once a year the taxman will want to see them. Some people hate anything to do with accounts and bung everything in a shoe box for the accountant to sort out once a year.

Bad idea!

It's a bad idea for three primary reasons:

- You're possibly running the business without really knowing what the cash situation is looking like.
- It will cost you a fortune in time charges for the accountant to sort out a horrible pile of scraps of paper.
- When you want to sell the business, the purchasers may be as fastidious at looking at accounting records as hopefully you were.

With a little bit of discipline it's easy to run a simple cash book and filing system that will solve all these problems.

Computer programs

By far the best way to do your accounts is to run them on a computer program. A computer system will save you hours of hard slog once you have learnt to use it. All leading programs will automatically work out your VAT returns in seconds, whereas people stay up all night doing VAT because they do it manually. See Appendix 5 for details.

Keep documents in a filing system arranged along the lines described below for a manual system, so that the accountant or VAT inspector can easily check entries in the books against the original documents.

Manual system

If you cannot get to grips with an accounts program, or it's going to take time, then you will need to start off with a manual system. The main thing is to get a good filing system going, along with a day book.

Start ring binders to keep all your supplier invoices in date order. It is a good idea to keep separate binders for suppliers you use a lot.

If you issue invoices to trade customers, keep copies of the invoices you issue in date order. If you use tills, keep the daily till summaries by stapling them to a weekly sheet.

Keep a petty cash book where you log the small items paid for in cash and keep the receipts in date order in a binder. In the book, record what you bought as well as how much it cost.

In the day book, record all transactions not in the petty cash. In the plus column, put daily sales totals. In the minus column, record purchases, stating what they are – stock, equipment, etc.

The daily effort of doing this is negligible if you do it as you go along. It is only when it is left that it becomes a nightmare, not only because of the volume to catch up with, but also because pieces of paper that were obvious at the time may become a mystery months later.

Most stationers sell bookkeeping ledgers where it is all set out for you.

Audit

You will need to appoint an accountant to finalise your annual accounts and submit returns to the taxman.

If you have been taking advice from an accountant prior to buying the business, you have presumably developed a working relationship with him. However, check on what his charges will be before committing and compare these with other firms. The charges will usually be quoted as an hourly rate according to the status of the person working for you. The basic work will be done by someone relatively junior, with a partner, whose time will be more expensive, checking the final result and signing off the accounts for the firm.

Chapter 18:

Insurances

There are insurances you must have, and a number of insurances you should seriously consider, business and personal.

Business insurances

Where do you go to get business insurances?

The obvious answer is an insurance broker. However, there are many general insurance brokers who do not do commercial insurance, so you will need to find one who does.

There are many insurance companies who have specialised insurance packages for particular types of business, and you need a broker who is familiar with your particular trade.

Clearly the vendor will be able to tell you where he gets his insurance, but it may also be worthwhile asking your accountant who might have other clients in the same business as you, and indeed you could ask other business owners not directly in competition with you.

What insurances are available?

If you buy a comprehensive policy the following will all be able to be included:

EMPLOYER'S LIABILITY

If you are employing staff this is a legal must and, by law, your certificate of cover must be displayed somewhere where all employees can see it. It covers you for claims from employees for accidents, negligence, etc.

PUBLIC LIABILITY

This is the same as you have in a typical home insurance policy. In the case of a business it is generally more important because you are exposed to visits by the general public.

LOSS OF PROFITS

If your shop burns down, you need to be covered by the buildings insurance to rebuild it. However, the problem is that you cannot trade and therefore cannot make a living. This cover provides income, based on the gross profit history of the business, so that you can continue to pay regular bills and take your personal drawings.

STOCK

Cover for loss of stock due to fire, flood, theft, etc.

Personal insurances

If you work for BT or BP, they may be inconvenienced if you cannot work for six months, but they will cover for you.

The fact is that in small businesses the owner/manager is critical – if you are not there, who is going to run it? The answer isn't, 'Well, the wife will.' Suppose for a moment you are both injured in a car accident!

It is essential to have some form of 'key man' insurance. 'Key man' insurance, as its name implies, provides money to pay a suitable person to run the business until you can get back.

If you arrange finance to purchase your business, the providers will almost certainly make it a condition that you have this cover unless they are well secured by bricks and mortar. It's fair enough. If the business is left unmanaged for a lengthy period, the value of the goodwill will soon evaporate. From your point of view the consideration is the same – would you like to see your investment evaporate whilst your two legs and an arm are in plaster? Insurance brokers who deal in life assurance can arrange this cover. If you arrange your business finance through a high street bank, they will almost certainly insist on this cover and they will want to arrange it for you.

I know that to most of us, including your scribe, insurance is a bore. But this is one you definitely need.

Appendix 1:

Self-assessment Questionnaire

The following questions and answers are designed to make you think about whether you are suited to running a business and whether your circumstances are appropriate.

There are no right or wrong answers as such and the questions are in no particular order. Think about your answers carefully and choose the answer to each question truthfully.

Although this is set out like a quiz, with indicative scores shown beside each answer, the main point of the exercise is not really about scoring. It is about prompting you to think about the key attributes you need to be successful in business, and making a realistic assessment of your abilities.

Question 1: How good are you at making decisions?

a) Normally I am very decisive. (20)
b) I can be decisive, but like to check with others if possible. (10)
c) I always like to check with others first. (5)
d) I never willingly take decisions without a lot of umm'ing and ah'ing. (-10)

Comments

If you answered a) then this is excellent, because in business you must be decisive. If you answered d) then you are definitely going to have to change, unless your partner can take decisions for you. If you answered b) or c) you should bear in mind that in business you often have to make quick decisions. It's always nice to be able to refer for a second opinion, but you must be prepared to decide on your own if time does not permit.

Question 2: Have you been involved in running a business before?

a) Yes. (10)
b) No. (0)

Comments

If yes, then good, you will have a fair idea of what you are letting yourself in for. If no, then don't worry as such. It doesn't matter, as long as you have a positive and logical approach to things and can truthfully claim to possess the attributes highlighted in this questionnaire.

Question 3: Are you willing and able to learn?

a) Yes. (10)
b) No. (-20)

Comments

If you answered no, then in that case you should not be going into business. We all have a lot to learn when we go into a new business, even if we have run businesses before.

Question 4: Is your spouse/partner supportive of your intention to buy a business?

a) Fully. (15)
b) Not fully, but not against. (10)
c) Not really in favour, but would not stop you. (5)
d) Totally against. (-20)

Comments

If a) then this is an excellent start. To have a fully supportive partner is bound to take off some of the pressure. If the answer is d) then you should not proceed unless you can change the situation through discussion. If you answered b) or c) you definitely should try to increase the level of support if possible by adapting your plans to meet the fears or objections. If you cannot do that, you must think very carefully before going ahead.

Question 5: How well do you react under pressure?

a)	I never or rarely get flustered.	(10)
b)	Sometimes it gets to me.	(5)
c)	It gets to me most of the time.	(-5)
d)	It always gets to me.	(-10)

Comments

Almost all business owners frequently feel under pressure of one type or another. If you were unable to answer a) or b) you must seriously doubt your ability to cope with pressure and you should think very carefully whether you should consider running a business of your own.

Question 6: How do you approach problem solving?

a)	I usually have a cool logical approach and reach a timely solution, if necessary with advice.	(20)
b)	I usually seek advice first before reaching a solution, but always face up to a problem.	(10)
c)	I tend to put it off as long as possible.	(-10)
d)	I have a habit of ignoring problems in the hope they will solve themselves or go away.	(-15)

Comments

If you answered a) or b) then good, but you must be able to make up your mind if advice is not readily available, as so many business problems need swift action.

If you answered c) or d) then think very carefully. In business you can't put things off – they nearly always get worse or lead to other problems, and problems never go away. You will need to change if you are to go ahead.

Question 7: Do you foresee running your own business to be hard work or less work for more reward?

a) I believe it will be hard work with the possibility of higher rewards.   (15)

b) I expect to work the same as before but with higher rewards.   (10)

c) I expect to be able to work less for at least the same rewards.   (0)

d) I am going into business because I want to work less hard than I have as an employee.   (-15)

Comments

If you answered a) you are most likely correct. Although the rewards can be higher than working for someone else, most business people will tell you that you have to work very hard.

Those who answered b) could be right, but the likelihood is that you will work much harder, especially in the early days.

If you answered c) or d) maybe, if you are lucky, it might turn out that way, but most business people work harder than they did when they were employees, and for longer hours. However, in most cases your answer is not a good basis upon which to decide to go into business, unless it is the type of business where you can do it on a part-time basis. If it is a full-time business you must assume you will be working very hard.

Question 8: How good are you at dealing with people?

a) I am confident dealing with people from all walks of life.   (20)

b) I am confident with people at my own level or below, but can be nervous with more important people.   (10)

c) I am good at dealing with people in my own sphere, but find it more difficult to communicate effectively with people from other backgrounds.   (10)

d) I am not a good communicator.   (-20)

Comments

In almost any business you are going to need to deal with people, unless it is Internet sales or something similar.

If you were able to answer a) then this is excellent because running a small business means you are a generalist and, in most instances, you will need to learn to communicate with all sorts of people.

If you answered b) or c) then you will need to develop your communication skills more broadly. For most people this should not be a problem. Many of us are nervous of people we see as important, but in business you will need to gain in confidence in front of people such as the bank manager or big customers, so that you give them confidence in you.

If you answered d) then unless you can overcome this problem you should seriously consider whether you should proceed with running your own business. As an employee, doing a specific job you can often get by without communication skills, but customers expect a business owner to be personable.

Question 9: Are you able to keep an open mind?

a)   Yes, I am always open to suggestions from anyone.   (10)
b)   I am open to suggestions from the right people.   (5)
c)   I am prepared to listen when I have asked for advice.   (5)
d)   I always want it done my way.   (-5)

Comment

Even billionaire businessmen listen to others and will admit that they are not always the best judges. Always be prepared to listen to anyone; sometimes the best ideas or solutions can come from the most unlikely people – even the office junior. It is good motivation for your employees if you always give them a hearing.

If you answered d) this is definitely something to think about carefully.

Question 10: Are you good at handling money?

a)   Yes, and I always plan ahead.   (20)
b)   Yes, but I take each day as it comes.   (5)
c)   I leave it to others.   (0)
d)   No, I put off thinking about it as long as possible.   (-20)

Comments

Lack of financial control and planning is one of the biggest reasons for business failures.

It is always vital in business that someone is keeping a close eye on the finances. If this is going to be you yourself, or your partner, and you were able to answer a) then this is the best possible approach.

If you answered b), a watchful approach is fine, but you do need to look ahead in business to ensure that the funds are there to pay the invoices, VAT, etc., when they become due.

If you answered c) then whilst bookkeepers or accountants can advise, they cannot be expected to watch over everything on their own, so you must learn to take an interest if you are to go into business.

If you answered d) there are many people like you, but you have a major change of approach to achieve if you are to go into business. You will at least need to make sure that you have someone competent watching the finances for you on a frequent basis, and you must take a regular interest.

Final summary and conclusions

As stated at the beginning of the questionnaire, the important aspect of going through the questions is the in-depth self-assessment it should provoke you to undertake. If you were genuinely able to answer a) to each question then you would have given yourself a maximum mark of 150. In that case you certainly have all the attributes needed to be a sound small business proprietor.

It would be nonsense to say that there is a pass mark. Obviously, if you gave yourself a very low overall score you will need to consider very carefully whether owning a business is for you. We are all different and it is not for everyone, so there is no need to feel bad if you have come to this conclusion. Indeed, if you do decide not to go ahead, you have taken a very positive step which should enable you to make a more appropriate move for you than going into business would have been. You will have probably saved yourself from a lot of unhappiness in the future.

If, like most of us, you have realised as a result of running through the questionnaire that you have many good points, but there are one or two areas that you need to think about, then at least you can do that before you decide what type of business to buy, and when.

Appendix 2:

Typical Gross Profit Margins

		% of sales
RETAIL & SERVICE		
Hairdresser		90
Dry Cleaner		85
Greetings Cards		50
Pet Shop		35
Fashion		35
Toys		25
Shoes/Clothing/Children's Wear		30–35
Hardware		30
Health Food		30
Greengrocer		30
Butcher		25
Bread/Patisserie/Confectionery		25
Newsagent (average mix)		22
newspapers, etc.	27	
confectionery	25	
tobacco	9	
Off Licence (average mix)		20
wines/beers	20–25	
soft drinks	25	
spirits	10	
tobacco	9	
General Stores		17–20
Petrol Stations		20–22
CATERING		
Bed & Breakfast		80
Fast Food		70
(after deducting sales staff costs)		50–55
Licensed Restaurant		60–65
Café/Sandwich Bar		55
Fish & Chips		50
Pub (wet sales)		45–50

Appendix 3:

Typical YPs

YEAR'S PURCHASE (YPs) – LEASEHOLD

	YP	Weeks t/over
Retail & Service		
Post Office	2.75*	n/a
Newsagent	2.5	15
Cards/Gifts	2.5	12–15
Off-Licence	2.0	12
Dry Cleaners	1.75–2.0	45
Gen. Stores/Health Foods	1.75	10
Hardware/Pets/Misc.	1.5	n/a
Greengrocer/Butcher/Fishmonger	1.0	10
Hairdresser	1.0	15
Fashions	0.75–1.0	n/a
Contract cleaning, etc.	.75	n/a
Catering		
Fish & Chips – all take away	2.5–3.0	35–40
– with restaurant	2.0–2.5	25–30
Fast Food	2.0–2.5	30–35
Café/Sandwich Bar	2.0–2.5	30
Licensed Restaurant	1.5–2.0	25

*2.75 times Post Office salary, assuming other retail sales break even. Add/deduct profits/losses from other retail sales at appropriate YP.

YPs for other businesses

The list includes the types of businesses most commonly bought and sold. Because these businesses change hands so frequently, and because they have fairly standard profit margins, it is possible to state normal YPs.

Other businesses vary widely – often even within the same sector. For example, a computer shop relying entirely on retail sales and repairs is different from one that has a substantial client list of local businesses supported under contract.

It is not, therefore, possible to produce a comprehensive list. All you can do is what the agent will have done – look for comparables, i.e. the most recent sales of similar businesses. To do this you will undoubtedly need to speak to a number of agents. Generally speaking, agents do not mind discussions like this, which is all part of the job.

For as many similar businesses as possible, find out when the sale occurred, what the nature of the business was and the YP. The agent will probably discuss with you the factors that went into why that YP was paid. You will then need to compare your business with the comparables you have and form a view. Let's take our computer shop example. The comparables you get are:

	Business A	Business B	Business C
Sold	3 yrs ago	1 yr ago	6 months ago
Business	retail 70% business clients 30%	retail only	business clients
YP	3.5	1.5	2.0

The business you are looking at is 50 per cent retail and 50 per cent business clients.

Hopefully you would find more than three comparables, but possibly not. Business A is a poor comparable that should be ignored. The 3.5 YP is way out of line with the others and, as it was three years ago, it is far too long ago to use unless there are no comparables that are more recent. Even then, it is retail, and you would expect it to be within the range of YPs appearing on our list.

Business B is entirely retail and Business C commercial. Your target business is 50/50 so the appropriate YP is probably the average.

Having now reached a reasoned conclusion you can go back to the selling agent to discuss the issue with him. He may agree or he may come up with compelling reasons why you are not right.

As always with valuation, there is no clear-cut right and wrong. If the situation is complex, or if the sums involved are considerable, take professional advice.

Appendix 4:

Useful Contacts

Whilst every care has been taken to ensure contact details are correct at the time of going to print, naturally these may be subject to change over time.

GENERAL BUSINESS ADVISORS

British Chambers of Commerce
65 Petty France
St James Park
London
SW1H 9EU
Tel: 020 7654 5800
www.chamberonline.co.uk

Junior Chamber International United Kingdom (JCI UK)
PO Box 6638
Grantham
NG31 9BX
Tel: 01476 404005
http://jciuk.org.uk

Business Link
Link House, 1st Floor
292–308 Southbury Road
Enfield
London
EN1 1TS

The above address is the London branch. Details of local offices can also be found on the website www.businesslink.gov.uk and from ringing 0845 600 9006.

Federation of Small Businesses
Sir Frank Whittle Way
Blackpool Business Park
Blackpool
Lancashire
FY4 2FE
Tel: 01253 336000
www.fsb.org.uk

The Prince's Trust
18 Park Square East
London
NW1 4LH
Tel: 020 7543 1234
www.princes-trust.org.uk

FINANCE

The Factors and Discounters Association (FDA)
Boston House, The Little Green
Richmond, Surrey
TW9 1QE
Tel: 020 8332 9955
www.factors.org.uk

PROFESSIONAL BODIES

British Franchise Association Ltd (BFA)
Thames View, Newtown Road
Henley-on-Thames
Oxfordshire
RG9 1HG
Tel: 01491 578050
www.british-franchise.org

Chartered Institute of Marketing
Moor Hall, Cookham
Maidenhead
Berkshire
SL6 9QH
Tel: 01628 427500
www.cim.co.uk

Institute of Chartered Accountants in England & Wales
Chartered Accountants' Hall
PO Box 433
London
EC2P 2BJ
Tel: 020 7920 8100
www.icaew.co.uk

Institute of Chartered Accountants in Ireland
11 Donegall Square South
Belfast
BT1 5JE
Tel: 028 9032 1600
www.icai.ie

Institute of Chartered Accountants of Scotland
CA House
21 Haymarket Yards
Edinburgh
EH12 5BH
Tel: 0131 347 0100
www.icas.org.uk

Law Society of England & Wales
113 Chancery Lane
London
WC2A 1PL
Tel: 020 7242 1222
www.lawsociety.org.uk

Law Society of Scotland
26 Drumsheugh Gardens
Edinburgh
EH3 7YR
Tel: 0131 226 7411
www.lawscot.org.uk

GOVERNMENT

ACAS
www.acas.org.uk

National Federation of Enterprise Agencies
12 Stephenson Court, Fraser Road
Priory Business Park
Bedford
MK44 3WH
Tel: 01234 831623
www.nfea.com

Business Eye in Wales
www.businesseye.org.uk

If you are looking to start your own business or for help with your existing small- or medium-sized business, then make contact through the website or on the low-cost phone number 08457 96 97 98 or by walking into one of the 32 centres across Wales.

Companies House
www.companieshouse.gov.uk

Department of Trade & Industry
1 Victoria Street
London
SW1H 0ET
Tel: 020 7215 5000
www.dti.gov.uk

HM Revenue and Customs
Tax
www.inlandrevenue.gov.uk
See Yellow Pages for the nearest office.

VAT
www.hmce.gov.uk
National General Enquiries line: 0845 010 9000

Highlands and Islands Enterprise

HIE's activities include: provision of business support services, delivery of training and learning programmes, assistance for community and cultural projects and measures for environmental renewal. These activities are primarily delivered by ten local enterprise companies (LECs).

Tel: 01463 234171

www.hie.co.uk

Business Gateway for Lowland Scotland

Starting up, or developing your business? The Business Gateway provides a single point of access to a range of integrated services offering assistance for business information, business start-up and business growth.

Tel: 0845 609 6611

www.bgateway.com

Appendix 5:

Computer Programs

There are a number of leading accounting programs on the market, starting at around £100, including amongst others:

Sage

Sage have a number of packages from beginner to advanced. Accountants like Sage because it links in neatly with the computerised accountants' programs they use for preparing the final accounts.

QuickBooks

QuickBooks is my personal favourite because it is very well documented, the terminology used is non-technical, and the set-up wizard to start off your file is very comprehensive and easy to understand. In my view, QuickBooks is the easiest for the newcomer to bookkeeping, and it is no wonder it has such a high share of the small business market.

TAS

TAS is another very good, relatively easy-to-use system that has been around many years.

Whichever program you choose, remember the cardinal rule: BACK-UP DATA REGULARLY AND KEEP THE BACK-UP DISKS IN A FIRE-PROOF PLACE.

Index

RIGHT WAY
PUBLISHING POLICY

HOW WE SELECT TITLES

RIGHT WAY consider carefully every deserving manuscript. Where an author is an authority on his subject but an inexperienced writer, we provide first-class editorial help. The standards we set make sure that every **RIGHT WAY** book is practical, easy to understand, concise, informative and delightful to read. Our specialist artists are skilled at creating simple illustrations which augment the text wherever necessary.

CONSISTENT QUALITY

At every reprint our books are updated where appropriate, giving our authors the opportunity to include new information.

FAST DELIVERY

We sell **RIGHT WAY** books to the best bookshops throughout the world. It may be that your bookseller has run out of stock of a particular title. If so, he can order more from us at any time – we have a fine reputation for "same day" despatch, and we supply any order, however small (even a single copy), to any bookseller who has an account with us. We prefer you to buy from your bookseller, as this reminds him of the strong underlying public demand for **RIGHT WAY** books. However, you can order direct from us by post, by phone with a credit card, or through our web site.

FREE

If you would like an up-to-date list of all **RIGHT WAY** and **RIGHT WAY PLUS** titles currently available, please send a stamped self-addressed envelope to:

ELLIOT RIGHT WAY BOOKS, BRIGHTON ROAD, LOWER KINGSWOOD, TADWORTH, SURREY, KT20 6TD, U.K. or visit our web site at www.right-way.co.uk